AF491337

Author's Note
By Ankit Sharma, Co-founder of All India EV

As I sit down to write this note, I find myself reflecting on the incredible journey this book has taken me on—a journey through India's complex energy landscape, its aspirations, and the urgent need for a secure, sustainable future. India's Quest for Energy Security is more than just a book; it is a manifestation of my deep-rooted passion for renewable energy, electric vehicles, and India's path toward self-reliance in the energy sector.

The world is changing at an unprecedented pace, and so is India's energy demand. As we move forward, energy security is no longer a topic confined to policy makers or industry insiders—it is an issue that touches every citizen. From the air we breathe to the electricity that powers our homes, India's energy choices will shape the future of our country, its economy, and its people. I wrote this book to not only explore these pressing issues but to spark a conversation that includes all of us, because we are all stakeholders in this journey.

At All India EV, our focus has always been on promoting cleaner, smarter transportation solutions. But my involvement in the EV sector made it increasingly clear that energy security doesn't exist in silos. It is interlinked with innovation, geopolitics, policy, and even the everyday choices we make as individuals. With each chapter, I hope to show the intricate web that binds these elements and the opportunities that arise from tackling our energy challenges head-on.

The inspiration behind this book stems from the people and industries that are driving India toward a greener future—engineers, entrepreneurs, policy makers, and everyday citizens alike. It is their collective will that will determine whether India can emerge as a global leader in clean energy, or whether we will remain reliant on outdated, environmentally damaging systems.

In this book, I have walked you through India's current energy landscape, explored new technologies like green hydrogen, and discussed the role of public-private partnerships and socio-economic impacts of this energy transition. But perhaps the most important message I want to leave you with is this: our journey does not end here. By 2044 and beyond, India has the opportunity to transform its energy systems entirely, leading to cleaner air, more resilient infrastructure, and better quality of life for all.

To my readers, I encourage you to keep questioning, keep learning, and most importantly, keep acting. Our energy future is not a distant dream—it's a reality that we are building right now. Every solar panel installed, every electric vehicle purchased, every energy-efficient light bulb switched on brings us closer to a secure, sustainable India.

Acknowledgement

First and foremost, my deepest gratitude goes to my family. To my parents and my brother, for their unwavering belief in me and their unconditional love and support throughout my life. You've always been my guiding light, and without you, this book would have never come to fruition

Now, to the amazing people who have been my pillars of strength and wisdom along this journey:

Rohit, my dear friend from our days at Inverted Energy, thank you for your constant friendship and encouragement.

To my wife, Kamini, the love of my life—your unwavering support, both personally and professionally, has been the fuel that kept me going.

A big thanks to Dr. Charusmita, Director of Statcon Energiaa, for your incredible friendship and expertise, and Saswat Panda, RE-100 Program Manager at The Climate Group, for your invaluable insights and collaboration.

My deepest gratitude also goes to my mentors, Deepak Gadhia Sir and Surya Jeedigunta, who have shaped my vision and provided guidance throughout my career.

Finally, I dedicate this book to my brother from the industry, Krishna Kaushik, who left us two years ago. This is for you, my friend. Your memory continues to inspire me every day, and I hope this book reflects the passion and dedication you had for the industry.

With heartfelt appreciation to everyone who has been part of this journey, this book is a tribute to your guidance, support, and friendship.

Let's explore the India's Quest
for Energy Security

It was April 25, 2024, and Ankit was in his office working on the monthly edition of All India EV. Across from him, Arun, the Head of Digital Marketing, was analyzing some stats from their latest campaign.

Hey, Ankit, Arun said, looking up with a grin. Looks like we're about to hit that milestone we've been talking about for ages. And the best part? It's happening sooner than we thought!"

Ankit smiled, appreciating the progress. That's great news, Arun. So, what do you think? Once we hit this milestone, what's next? Any ideas on the next big thing?

Arun leaned back, thinking for a moment. Well, I was about to ask you the same thing. What's the next milestone for All India EV?

Ankit paused, then said, "Actually, I've been thinking… What if the next big project isn't just about the platform, but something different? Like… a book."

A book? Arun raised an eyebrow, intrigued. That sounds amazing! I mean, you've already written poetry, short stories, and long articles, so writing a book feels like the natural next step. What kind of book are you thinking?

Ankit shook his head. Not fiction this time. I'm thinking about a technical book. Something that dives deep into our industry. I want to write about India's roadmap to achieving energy security.

Arun tilted his head, curious. Energy security? I've heard about net zero and carbon neutrality, but energy security is new to me. What exactly does that mean?

Good question, Ankit said, leaning forward. More than 45% of our energy comes from coal and oil imports. That makes us dependent on other countries. If those countries decide to cut us off, it could cause a huge problem for us.

Arun nodded thoughtfully. Wow, that sounds ambitious, but I get it. Considering we're the third-largest power consumer in the world, it's something we need to work on. But has India already started on this path?

Absolutely, Ankit said confidently. We've made great strides with policies that encourage EV adoption, delicense energy selling, push for standalone energy storage systems, and promote green hydrogen and ethanol. The groundwork is already there.

"Then what are you waiting for? Arun smiled. This book sounds like it's going to be important. You should start working on it.

Ankit hesitated for a moment. But...

But what? Arun asked, sensing Ankit's hesitation.

I'm not sure if I have the expertise to cover the entire energy sector," Ankit admitted. "It's a massive topic, and I don't know if I can pull it off alone.

Arun gave a reassuring smile. You don't have to do it alone. You've got a network of experts around you. Why not reach out for help?

Who do you think I should ask? Ankit asked.

Well, you've got Kamini for the solar industry, Rohit for ESS and EVs,   Dr. Charusmita for green hydrogen, and of course, your mentor Gadhia Sir. He's a walking social network—he can connect you with the right people.

Ankit's face brightened. You're right. That's a solid plan. Thanks, Arun, I feel a lot better about this now.

Anytime Arun said. Now, when do I get to see the outline?

Introduction to "India's Quest for Energy Security"

India is at a pivotal juncture in its energy journey, balancing the demands of rapid economic growth, a rising population, and the urgent need to transition toward sustainable and secure energy systems.

The energy sector forms the backbone of the country's development, influencing everything from industrial growth and infrastructure development to rural electrification and poverty alleviation.

This book, "India's Quest for Energy Security," provides a comprehensive exploration of India's energy landscape in 2024 and offers a forward-looking perspective on the country's roadmap to achieving energy security by 2044 and future.

We will examine how India's energy requirements vary across its diverse regions, its evolving power generation mix, the rise of renewable energy, and the role of emerging technologies like electric vehicles (EVs), green hydrogen, and battery energy storage systems (BESS).

Additionally, we will delve into India's geopolitical energy relationships and its participation in global climate and energy alliances.

This book is intended to serve as a comprehensive resource for understanding where India currently stands in its energy transition, the challenges that lie ahead, and the strategies and innovations that will shape its future.

By 2044, India envisions a secure, resilient, and sustainable energy system, where its energy needs are met not only throughB domestic innovation but also through international cooperation and environmental stewardship.

Join me as we explore India's past, present, and future in the energy sector, unpacking the intricate details that will determine the country's energy security and, consequently, its economic security.

Table of Content

Ankit: So, Arun, what do you think of the outline and the introduction so far?

Arun: Wow, this is really solid. The outline looks comprehensive—you've covered everything. From power generation to storage, transmission, even maintenance and consumption. You've definitely left no stone unturned. It's really shaping up into something significant.

Ankit: Glad to hear that. I've been trying to think of everything that's critical to energy security.

Arun: It shows. The way you've structured it makes it easy to follow, too. So, what's the next step?

Ankit: Well, the next part is simple getting started with the writing.

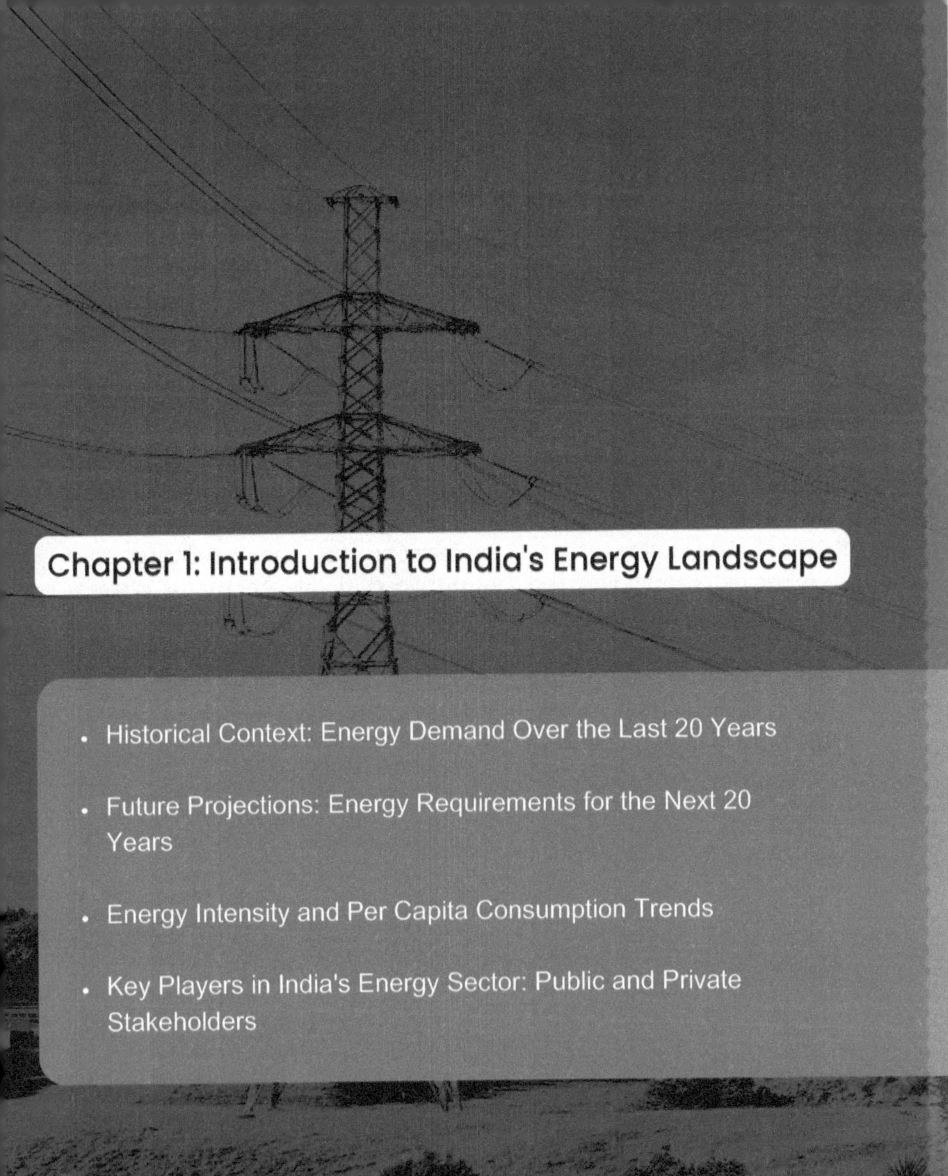

Chapter 1: Introduction to India's Energy Landscape

- Historical Context: Energy Demand Over the Last 20 Years

- Future Projections: Energy Requirements for the Next 20 Years

- Energy Intensity and Per Capita Consumption Trends

- Key Players in India's Energy Sector: Public and Private Stakeholders

India's energy landscape is undergoing a transformative shift as the nation grapples with its growing energy demands.

As the world's third-largest energy consumer, India's rapid industrialization, urbanization, and expanding population are driving a surge in energy consumption.

This chapter explores the evolution of India's energy needs over the past two decades, the ongoing reliance on traditional energy sources like coal and oil, and the increasing prominence of renewable energy.

It also delves into future projections for the country's energy requirements, outlining the key public and private sector players in this critical industry.

With a focus on energy security, sustainability, and economic growth, India's pursuit of a balanced energy strategy is set to define its trajectory in the 21st century.

Overview of India's Growing Energy Needs

India's energy demand continues to rise, reflecting the country's rapid industrialization, urbanization, and growing population.

As of **March 2025**, India remains the world's third-largest energy consumer, with primary energy consumption reaching approximately **37.8 quadrillion BTUs**, up from **17 quadrillion BTUs in 2000**.

This sustained growth highlights India's emergence as a major global economic player, driven by a population exceeding 1.43 billion and increasing energy needs for sectors like manufacturing, services, and transportation.

India's energy security remains a critical priority as the country seeks to reduce its dependence on imported fossil fuels. India imports about 84% of its crude oil and 48% of its natural gas.

To mitigate this, the **National Energy Policy (NEP)** emphasizes a push toward renewable energy sources, with significant investments in solar, wind, and bioenergy, along with improvements in energy efficiency.

Historical Context: Energy Demand Over the Last 20 Years

India's energy landscape has undergone a profound transformation over the past two decades. Since 2000, the country's energy demand has **grown by nearly 82%**, spurred by a high GDP growth rate of around 6.8% annually during this period.

- Coal: India continues to rely heavily on coal, which made up around **41.5% of its total energy consumption**, down slightly from 42% in 2024 due to the gradual shift toward renewables. In 2025, India consumed approximately 955 million tons of coal, up from 350 million tons in 2000.

- Oil: India remains the **third-largest oil consumer globally**, with daily consumption rising to **5.7 million barrels per day** (bpd) in 2025, driven mainly by the transportation and industrial sectors. Over 84% of the oil is imported, making it a major vulnerability for the country.

- Natural Gas: Natural gas consumption has steadily increased, reaching 66 billion cubic meters (bcm) in 2025, up from 20 bcm in 2000. This growth is driven by rising industrial demand and government initiatives to transition to a gas-based economy.

- Renewables: Renewable energy now contributes around 24.1% of India's total energy mix, a dramatic increase from less than 2% in 2000. As of March 2025, India's installed renewable energy capacity stood at 174 GW, with solar (85 GW) and wind (52 GW) making the largest contributions.

In addition, India achieved full household electrification in 2019 through initiatives like the Saubhagya scheme, significantly improving access to electricity across rural and urban areas.

Future Projections: Energy Requirements for the Next 20 Years

India's energy needs are expected to nearly double by 2045, as continued economic growth, urbanization, and industrialization fuel demand. By 2045, India's energy demand is forecasted to surpass 57 quadrillion BTUs, according to the International Energy Agency (IEA).

Electricity: **Demand for electricity is projected to triple by 2045**, driven by rising standards of living, widespread electrification, and the adoption of electric vehicles (EVs). India's installed power capacity may need to increase from around 450 GW in 2025 to 950 GW by 2045, with renewables expected to account for over 52% of total capacity.

Renewables: India is expected to achieve its ambitious target of 500 GW of renewable energy capacity by 2030, with solar and wind power leading the way. **By 2045**, renewables are anticipated to make up over **52%** of India's electricity generation capacity.

Oil: Despite the global push toward cleaner energy, India's oil demand is projected to increase to 7.5 million bpd by 2045, driven by the aviation, transport, and petrochemical sectors.

Natural Gas: The share of natural gas in India's energy mix is expected to grow from 6.1% in 2025 to around 15% by 2045, with government policies promoting cleaner fuels for industrial and residential uses.

Coal: Although coal's share in the energy mix is expected to decline, it will continue to play a significant role, particularly in power generation, due to the slow transition away from coal-based energy production.

Energy Intensity and Per Capita Consumption Trends

India has made substantial progress in improving its energy efficiency. The country's energy intensity—measured as the amount of energy consumed per unit of GDP—has decreased from 0.58 tons of oil equivalent per thousand USD in 2000 to 0.39 in 2025.

This decline is attributed to the adoption of energy-efficient technologies, increased reliance on renewables, and government-led energy-saving programs.

- Per Capita Energy Consumption: IIn 2025, India's per capita energy consumption was around 975 kilograms of oil equivalent (kgoe), still lower than the global average of 1,500 kgoe. By 2045, per capita consumption is expected to rise to about 1,630 kgoe as more people gain access to modern energy services, living standards improve, and the adoption of energy-intensive technologies, like EVs, increases

Key Players in India's Energy Sector: Public and Private Stakeholders

India's energy sector comprises major public and private entities that are pivotal to its development.

Public Sector:

- **Coal India Limited (CIL):** The world's largest coal producer, accounting for about 77% of India's coal production in 2025.

- **Oil and Natural Gas Corporation (ONGC):** Responsible for 64% of domestic oil and gas production, ONGC continues to be a key player in India's energy landscape.

- **Indian Oil Corporation (IOC) and Bharat Petroleum Corporation Limited (BPCL):** Together, they refine over 54% of India's crude oil, making them major players in the downstream oil industry.

- **NTPC Limited:** India's largest power producer, generating nearly 17% of the country's electricity, primarily from coal.

Private Sector:

- Reliance Industries: The conglomerate remains a key player in refining, oil, and gas exploration. It is also heavily investing in renewable energy, with plans to develop significant solar and hydrogen capacity.

- Adani Group: Adani is a leading player in coal mining, renewables, and power distribution, with its renewable energy arm becoming one of India's largest.

- Tata Power: Among the leading private power producers, with over 14 GW of installed capacity and a strong focus on renewables.

- ReNew Power and Azure Power: These companies are leading the renewable energy transition with significant investments in solar and wind energy projects.

International Players:

Global energy giants like BP, Shell, and Total Energy have increased their presence in India, particularly in renewables and LNG projects. Their partnerships with Indian firms reflect the country's growing importance in the global energy market.

India's energy landscape is at a critical juncture. The country must balance the need for continued economic growth with the global transition to cleaner energy.

In the coming decades, India will increasingly rely on renewable energy, improve energy efficiency, and reduce its dependence on imported fossil fuels.

Achieving its long-term energy security goals will require coordinated efforts across public and private sectors, as well as international collaborations.

Arun: Nice work, Ankit. This chapter looks solid! Honestly, it doesn't seem like you needed any help at all.

Ankit: Thanks, Arun. Appreciate that. By the way, Arun, if you don't mind me asking, what did you take away from this chapter? I'm curious to know your understanding of it.

Arun: From what I gathered, Chapter 1 gives a solid overview of India's current energy landscape. You've painted a clear picture of how India's energy demand has grown massively over the past two decades due to industrialization, urbanization, and population growth. It's amazing to see how the country has more than doubled its energy consumption since 2000, reaching 37.8 quadrillion BTUs in 2025.

You also highlighted how coal, oil, and natural gas still dominate India's energy mix, with coal accounting for nearly 41.5% of total consumption in 2025. But what really struck me was the growing role of renewables—how solar and wind have gone from almost nothing to now contributing 24.1% of the energy mix, with a target of 500 GW renewable capacity by 2030. That shows a huge shift toward cleaner energy.

Another key takeaway for me was the historical context—how India's energy demand has grown by 82% in the last 20 years—and the projections for the future. By 2045, energy demand could nearly double again, and electricity demand might even triple. It's clear that renewable energy, especially solar and wind, will play an essential role in meeting this future demand, though coal and oil will still be part of the mix for a while.

I also noticed the focus on energy intensity and per capita consumption. It's interesting to see how India has managed to improve energy efficiency over the years, reducing energy intensity while still growing economically.

And the per capita energy consumption of 975 kgoe in 2025 compared to the global average of 1,500 kgoe really puts things in perspective—there's still a long way to go as India develops.

Lastly, the way you outlined the key players in both the public and private sectors helped me understand who's driving the energy sector in India. Companies like Coal India, ONGC, Reliance, and Adani are shaping the landscape, and international players like Shell and Total Energies are increasingly involved, particularly in renewables.

New Chapter 2: Regional Energy Requirements and Market Trends

- Energy Demand by Region: Northern, Southern, Western, Eastern, and Northeastern India

- Rural vs. Urban Energy Demand Dynamics

- Industrial, Residential, and Commercial Energy Market Segments

- The Role of State Governments in Energy Policy and Infrastructure

- Key Players in India's Energy Sector: Public and Private Stakeholders

India's quest for energy security is deeply influenced by its vast and diverse geography. The country's energy needs vary significantly across regions, each defined by unique demographic, economic, and industrial characteristics.

In this chapter, we explore how regional energy demands shape India's energy landscape and examine the factors driving these disparities.

From the industrial hubs of the Western and Southern regions to the resource-rich yet underutilized potential of Eastern and Northeastern India, the country's energy map is marked by contrasts that highlight the challenges of ensuring energy access and sustainability.

Additionally, India's market is evolving rapidly due to increasing urbanization, rising incomes, and industrial growth, but regional disparities in power consumption and access remain critical issues to address.

Energy Demand by Region: Northern, Southern, Western, Eastern, and Northeastern India

India's energy landscape continues to be shaped by its vast geography and diverse regional requirements.

Each region—Northern, Southern, Western, Eastern, Central, and Northeastern India—presents unique energy demand patterns, influenced by demographic growth, industrial activity, and infrastructural development.

The country's overall energy consumption has risen steadily in recent years, crossing 37.8 quadrillion BTUs as of March 2025, driven by rapid urbanization, rising incomes, and the continued expansion of energy access. However, disparities in power access, demand dynamics between rural and urban regions, and the influence of state-level policies remain critical factors in shaping India's energy market.

Energy Demand by Region: Northern, Southern, Western, Eastern, Central, and Northeastern India

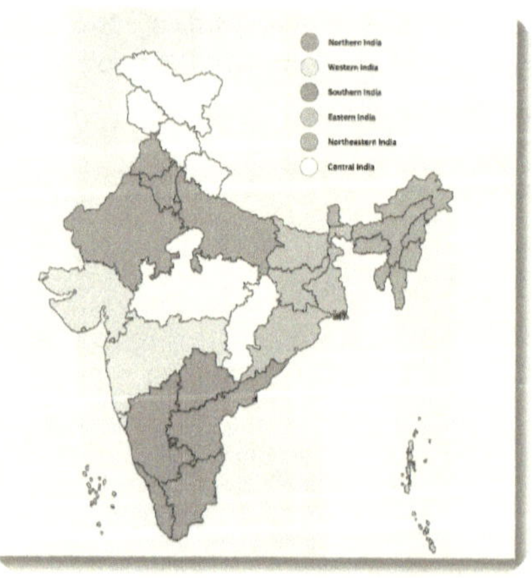

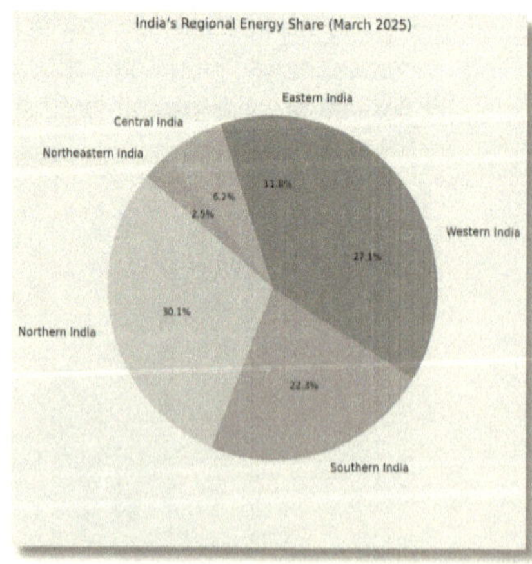

Northern India:

- Key States: Uttar Pradesh, Punjab, Haryana, Delhi, Rajasthan.

- Energy Demand:
  - Northern India remains the largest energy-consuming region, accounting for 30.1% of India's total electricity demand in 2025.
  - Uttar Pradesh, with its population exceeding 225 million, continues to be the region's largest energy consumer.
  - Delhi, as a major commercial hub, witnessed peak summer electricity demand reaching 8,100 MW in 2025, reflecting the growing energy needs of urban centers.
  - Punjab and Haryana's agriculture-driven demand also contributes significantly to the region's energy consumption.

Southern India:

- Key States: Tamil Nadu, Karnataka, Andhra Pradesh, Kerala, Telangana.

- Energy Demand:
  - Southern India, home to major industrial hubs and technology corridors, contributes 22.3% of India's electricity demand.
  - Tamil Nadu leads the region with strong renewable energy growth, particularly in wind and solar power.
  - Hyderabad has emerged as one of the fastest-growing urban centers for residential electricity demand, driven by rising middle-class incomes and increasing appliance penetration.

Western India:

- Key States: Maharashtra, Gujarat, Rajasthan, Goa.

- Energy Demand:
  - Western India retains its status as India's industrial powerhouse, accounting for 27.1% of total electricity demand.
  - Maharashtra alone consumes 13.3% of India's electricity, making it the largest single-state energy consumer in the country.
  - Gujarat, with its robust manufacturing and petrochemical industries, is another major contributor.

Eastern India:

- Key States: West Bengal, Bihar, Odisha, Jharkhand.

- Energy Demand:
  - Eastern India, despite its rich resource base in coal and minerals, continues to lag behind in energy consumption compared to the western and northern regions.
  - In 2025, it accounted for 11.8% of national electricity demand. However, industrial activities in states like Odisha—particularly steel production—are driving a gradual increase in energy requirements.

Central India:

- Key States: Madhya Pradesh & Chhattisgarh.

- Energy Demand:
  - Central India contributed around 6.2% of India's total electricity consumption as of March 2025.
  - Chhattisgarh, a key coal-producing state, supports heavy industries like steel and cement that are significant energy consumers.
  - Madhya Pradesh's energy demand has grown steadily, fueled by urbanization and expanding industrial and commercial sectors.

Northeastern India:

- Key States: Assam, Meghalaya, Tripura, Arunachal Pradesh, Manipur, Mizoram, Nagaland, Sikkim.

- Energy Demand:
  - The Northeastern region continues to have the lowest share in India's energy consumption, at 2.5% in 2025, due to its sparse population and limited industrial base.
  - However, infrastructure projects and expanding connectivity are beginning to stimulate demand. Assam remains the region's largest energy consumer.

Rural vs. Urban Energy Demand Dynamics

India's rural and urban energy consumption presents a sharp contrast:

Urban Areas: Urban regions continue to dominate electricity consumption, accounting for about 69% of the total demand in 2024-2025. Growing urbanization, the expansion of services, and middle-class households drive this demand, with increased usage of air conditioners, lighting, and appliances.

- Example: By March 2025, Mumbai's peak electricity demand reached 3,850 MW, while Delhi's summer demand surged to 8,100 MW.

Rural Areas: Despite significant government electrification initiatives, rural India, which houses over 64% of the population, consumes only about 22% of total electricity. Inconsistent access and lower industrial activity continue to contribute to this disparity.

- Example: Although nearly 100% village electrification was achieved, per capita electricity consumption in rural areas is still about one-fourth of urban India.

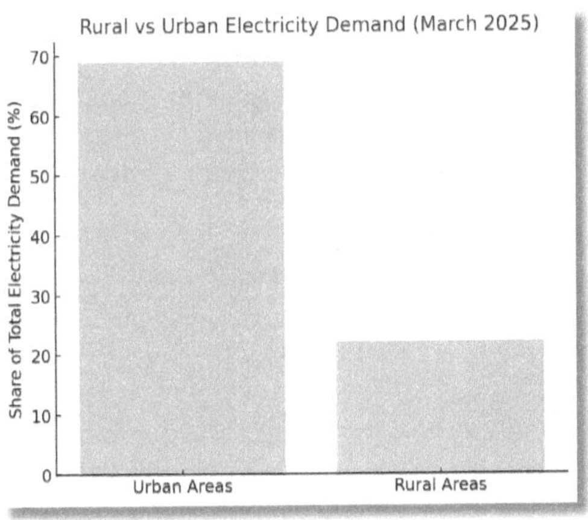

Industrial, Residential, and Commercial Energy Market Segments

Industrial Energy Demand:
The industrial sector remains the largest energy consumer, accounting for 45% of India's total electricity consumption in 2024-2025.

Example: The industrial electricity demand reached 670 TWh, with Maharashtra, Gujarat, and Tamil Nadu being the top energy-consuming states due to their strong manufacturing, petrochemical, and auto industry bases.

Residential Energy Demand:
Residential energy consumption accounts for about 31% of total demand, driven by rising household electrification and the proliferation of energy-hungry appliances like air conditioners, refrigerators, and washing machines.

Example: Residential electricity demand grew at a compound annual growth rate (CAGR) of 6.8% from 2000 to 2025, fueled by rising middle-class incomes and increased air-conditioning usage, particularly in urban areas.

Commercial Energy Demand:
The commercial sector, which includes offices, malls, and public infrastructure, contributes around 13% to total energy consumption. IT hubs like Bengaluru, Hyderabad, and Pune are key contributors.

Example: In 2024-2025, commercial sector energy demand saw a significant rise in cities like Bengaluru and Pune due to the growing office space footprint and the rapid expansion of the retail sector.

The Role of State Governments in Energy Policy and Infrastructure

State governments continue to play a pivotal role in shaping India's energy policies and driving infrastructure development across the country. Their involvement in electricity distribution, renewable energy promotion, and infrastructure investment is critical to meeting India's growing energy demand and addressing regional disparities.

State Electricity Boards (SEBs): SEBs remain central to electricity distribution but face persistent financial challenges in several states. As of 2025, reforms under the Revamped Distribution Sector Scheme (RDSS) have helped reduce aggregate technical and commercial (AT&C) losses in states like Gujarat and Tamil Nadu to below 15%, while states like Uttar Pradesh and Bihar continue to struggle with losses exceeding 28%.

Policy Initiatives: Progressive states like Gujarat, Karnataka, and Maharashtra have emerged as leaders in promoting renewable energy through innovative policy frameworks. Gujarat has achieved 24 GW of installed renewable capacity, and Karnataka remains a hub for rooftop solar projects.

Infrastructure Development: Several states have invested heavily in upgrading transmission and distribution networks. Maharashtra and Tamil Nadu, for instance, have adopted smart grid technologies to improve energy efficiency and reliability, while Rajasthan is investing in ultra-mega solar parks to harness its vast solar potential.

Despite progress, issues such as financial stress of SEBs, delays in renewable energy integration, and uneven implementation of central schemes persist in many states, particularly in Eastern and Northeastern regions.

Key Players in India's Energy Sector: Public and Private Stakeholders

India's energy market is shaped by dynamic participation from both public and private sector players across generation, transmission, and distribution. Together, they drive the country's efforts toward energy security, sustainability, and modernization.

Public Sector:

- NTPC Limited: Continues to be the largest power generator, contributing 23.8% of India's total installed capacity in 2025. NTPC is expanding into renewables, with over 6 GW of solar and wind projects commissioned.

- Power Grid Corporation of India (PGCIL): Remains the dominant player in electricity transmission, operating more than 175,000 circuit kilometers of transmission lines and integrating renewable energy into the grid.

- State Electricity Boards (SEBs): SEBs continue to play critical roles in electricity distribution. Financial and operational reforms under the Revamped Distribution Sector Scheme (RDSS) have improved performance in states like Gujarat and Tamil Nadu, but challenges remain in Bihar and Jharkhand.

Private Sector:

- Reliance Power and Adani Power: Major players in both thermal and renewable energy sectors. Reliance's clean energy initiatives include green hydrogen production, while Adani Power has scaled up renewable capacity with significant solar and wind investments.

- Tata Power: Leads in integrated energy solutions, from generation to distribution, and now operates over 4 GW of renewable energy capacity. Its focus on rooftop solar has made it a market leader in residential and commercial solar installations.

- ReNew Power and Adani Green Energy: Dominate the renewable energy landscape. As of 2025, ReNew Power operates 13 GW of renewable assets, while Adani Green Energy has achieved 28 GW of installed renewable capacity, nearing its target of 30 GW by mid-2025.

Although near-universal electricity access has been achieved in urban regions, rural areas—particularly in states like Bihar and Jharkhand—continue to face challenges with power reliability and supply consistency.

On the other hand, Gujarat and Tamil Nadu remain leaders in providing stable and high-quality electricity, thanks to robust grid infrastructure and effective state policies.

The national average per capita electricity consumption in 2024-2025 rose to approximately 1,310 kWh, reflecting rising incomes and urbanization.

However, stark disparities persist: states like Delhi (2,650 kWh) and Gujarat (2,520 kWh) far exceed this average, while states such as Bihar (280 kWh) and Assam (320 kWh) continue to lag behind.

India's energy sector is undergoing a transformative shift, shaped by regional needs, evolving policy frameworks, and technological innovations.

Addressing these regional disparities and accelerating renewable energy adoption will be critical to achieving the country's energy security and sustainability goals in the coming decades.

Arun: Hey Ankit, this chapter is pretty detailed. You've covered the regional energy needs across India really well. I'm impressed with how you've broken it down by region and highlighted the energy consumption patterns in each area.

Ankit: Thanks, Arun. I wanted to show that India's energy demand isn't uniform each region has its own unique challenges and growth trajectories.

Arun: Yeah, I noticed that. It's fascinating how places like Western India are so industrialized and consume a massive amount of energy, while regions like the Northeast still account for just 2.5% of total electricity demand. But even then, the gap is slowly closing as infrastructure projects and renewable energy initiatives drive growth there.

Ankit: Exactly, and that's why addressing these regional disparities is so critical if India wants to achieve energy security in the next two decades.

Arun: So, by the way, what's next after this?

Ankit: Next, I'll work on integrating the regional data further and then dive into the impact of state-level policies and reforms. There's still a lot more to explore. But before we move on, Arun, what did you take away from this chapter? I'm curious to know what stood out to you.

Arun: Well, what I understood is that India's energy needs are deeply shaped by its geography and regional differences. For example, Western and Southern India are industrial powerhouses, which explains their high energy consumptionMaharashtra alone consumes 13.3% of India's electricity. On the other hand, regions like the Northeast are catching up, thanks to ongoing infrastructure projects and government focus on connectivity.

Chapter 3: India's Power Generation Mix

- Current Power Generation: Coal, Gas, Hydro, Nuclear, and Renewables

- Transition to Renewable Energy: Solar, Wind, Biomass

- Fossil Fuels: Role of Coal and Oil in India's Energy Supply

- Nuclear Power: Present Capacity and Future Potential

- The Role of Private Sector and Public-Private Partnerships in Power Generation

India stands at a pivotal moment in its energy journey, reflecting both its growing demand and its ambitious sustainability goals.

As the nation progresses toward its 2030 targets, the power generation mix continues to evolve, balancing traditional fossil fuels with a rapidly expanding renewable energy sector.

As of March 2025, India's total installed power generation capacity reached approximately 452 GW, underscoring the complexities of this transition. Coal remains the backbone of India's electricity supply, contributing nearly 44.8% of installed capacity, but its share is gradually declining as renewables surge ahead.

The renewable energy sector, led by solar and wind, has witnessed record growth in recent years. Renewables now contribute 36.9% of India's total installed capacity, aligning with the country's commitment to combat climate change and reduce its carbon footprint.

This chapter provides an in-depth look at India's power generation infrastructure, analyzing each major energy source—from coal and gas to hydropower, nuclear, and renewables. It also examines the growing role of the private sector, public-private partnerships, and government initiatives driving the transition.

As India strives for energy security and sustainability, understanding this intricate blend of old and new energy sources is critical to envisioning its path forward in the coming decades.

Current Power Generation: Coal, Gas, Hydro, Nuclear, and Renewables

India's total installed power generation capacity stood at approximately **452 GW as of March 31, 2025**. The distribution of this capacity across various energy sources reflects the country's ongoing shift toward renewables, even as coal maintains its dominance as a reliable energy source.

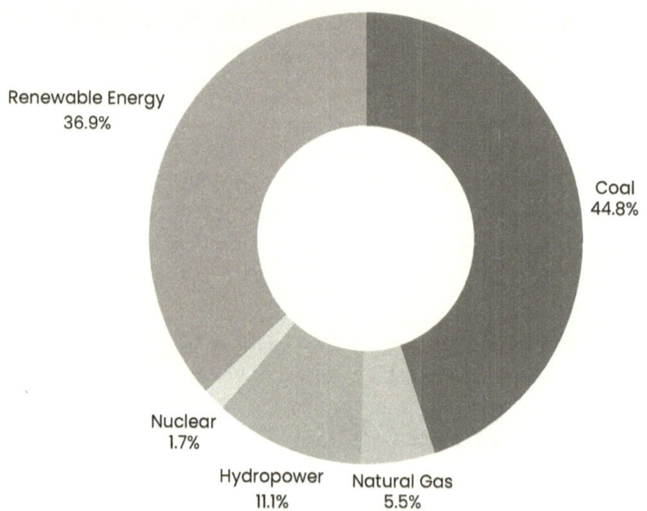

Coal

- Installed Capacity: 203 GW (~44.8% of total)
- Coal remains the largest contributor to India's power generation mix due to its domestic abundance and the reliability of thermal power plants. However, its share in the energy mix has seen a gradual decline as renewables grow rapidly.
- **2024-25 Contribution:** Coal-based electricity generation accounted for nearly 66% of India's total electricity output.

Natural Gas

- Installed Capacity: 25 GW (~5.5% of total)
- Gas-based power generation remains relatively stagnant due to high LNG import costs and limited domestic production. These plants are primarily used for peaking and backup power, particularly in regions with variable renewable energy penetration.

Hydropower

- Installed Capacity: 48 GW (~11% of total).
- Hydropower remains crucial for India's renewable energy portfolio, providing both electricity and grid balancing services. States like Himachal Pradesh, Uttarakhand, and Arunachal Pradesh continue to lead in hydropower capacity.
- 2023-24 Hydropower Contribution: Roughly 11-12% of the country's total electricity generation came from hydroelectric sources.

Nuclear

- Installed Capacity: 8 GW (~1.7% of total)
- Nuclear energy remains a small but critical component of India's power generation strategy. The Kudankulam and Tarapur nuclear plants continue as key contributors, and additional reactors such as Kakrapar-3 are under commissioning.
- **2024-25 Contribution:** Nuclear power provided approximately 3.6% of India's total electricity generation.

Renewables (Solar, Wind, Biomass):

- Installed Capacity: 167 GW (~36.9% of total)
- Renewables are the fastest-growing segment of India's power sector. As of March 2025:
    - Solar: 90 GW (primarily from large solar parks in Rajasthan and Gujarat).
    - Wind: 52 GW (led by Tamil Nadu, Gujarat, and Maharashtra).
    - Biomass and Small Hydro: Combined 25 GW.
- Renewables now account for over 36% of India's installed capacity, reflecting the government's strong push toward a low-carbon economy.

Transition to Renewable Energy: Solar, Wind, Biomass

India's renewable energy sector has maintained its rapid growth trajectory, positioning the country among the world's leaders in clean energy deployment. By **March 31, 2025**, renewable energy accounted for 36.9% of the total installed capacity, reflecting strong policy support and investment flows.

The government's commitment to achieving **500 GW of non-fossil fuel capacity by 2030** is driving this transition, supported by ambitious targets and technological advancements.

Solar Power:

- Installed Capacity: 90 GW (as of March 2025)
- Solar energy continues to be the cornerstone of India's renewable energy expansion. Mega solar parks such as the Bhadla Solar Park (Rajasthan) and Pavagada Solar Park (Karnataka) remain key contributors.
- Over the past five years, India has consistently added an average of 11 GW of solar capacity annually, reflecting both utility-scale and rooftop solar growth.
- **2030 Target:** India aims to achieve 280 GW of solar capacity as part of its renewable energy ambitions.

Wind Power:

- Installed Capacity: 52 GW (as of March 2025)
- Wind energy has shown steady growth, especially in coastal states such as Tamil Nadu, Gujarat, and Maharashtra. India remains the world's fourth-largest wind energy producer, supported by favorable policies and private sector investments.
- **2030 Target:** The goal is to increase wind capacity to 140 GW.

Biomass Power:

- Installed Capacity: 10 GW (as of March 2025)
- Biomass energy plays a crucial role in rural India, particularly in agricultural states like Punjab and Uttar Pradesh, where it supports both electricity generation and sustainable waste management.
- Future growth will depend on integrating biomass projects into decentralized rural energy systems.

Fossil Fuels: Role of Coal and Oil in India's Energy Supply

Fossil fuels remain an integral part of India's energy landscape, even as the country intensifies its push toward cleaner energy sources. Coal continues to be the backbone of electricity generation, while oil plays a critical role in industrial activity and transportation.

Coal:

- Contribution (2024-25): Coal-based power generation accounted for approximately **66% of India's total electricity output**, down slightly from **68% in 2023-24**, reflecting the gradual penetration of renewables.
- India remains the world's second-largest coal producer, with domestic coal production reaching **875 million tonnes in 2024-25**.
- Public sector enterprises such as Coal India Limited continue to dominate production, supplying fuel to thermal power plants across the country.

Oil:

- While oil is not a major fuel for electricity generation, it remains vital for India's industrial and transportation sectors.
- **2024-25 Oil Consumption:** India's oil demand stood at 5.5 million barrels per day (bpd), driven by rising vehicle ownership and industrial use.
- India imports approximately 84% of its crude oil needs, making diversification and energy security a policy priority.

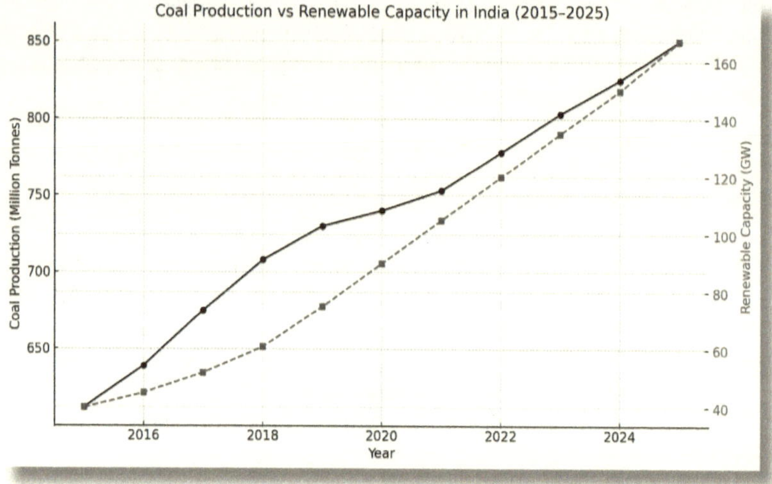

> As India works toward its net-zero target for 2070, reducing dependence on coal and oil is critical. However, in the near term, these fuels will continue to play a significant role in supporting economic growth and energy access.

Nuclear Power: Present Capacity and Future Potential

Nuclear energy continues to play a small but strategic role in India's power generation mix. While its share remains modest, nuclear power is critical for providing stable, low-carbon electricity as India works toward its long-term decarbonization goals.

- Installed Capacity as of March 2025: 8 GW (~1.7% of total)
- India's operational nuclear power plants are located in **Tamil Nadu (Kudankulam), Maharashtra (Tarapur), Rajasthan (Rawatbhata), and Gujarat (Kakrapar).**
- Nuclear power generation contributed approximately **3.6% of total electricity output** in 2024-25, producing ~43 TWh of electricity.

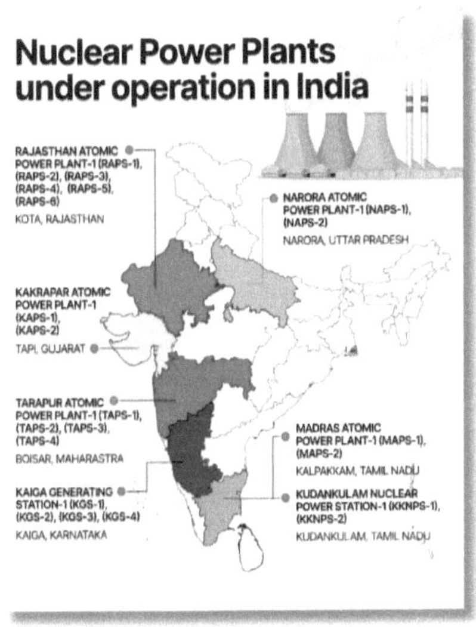

India has ambitious plans to expand its nuclear capacity to 22.5 GW by 2031, aiming to triple its current capacity over the next six years.

New Projects Underway:

- **Kakrapar Unit 3 (Gujarat):** Commissioning in progress.
- **Kudankulam Units 3 & 4 (Tamil Nadu):** Under construction and expected to be operational by 2027.
- Additional reactors are under development in Haryana and Andhra Pradesh.

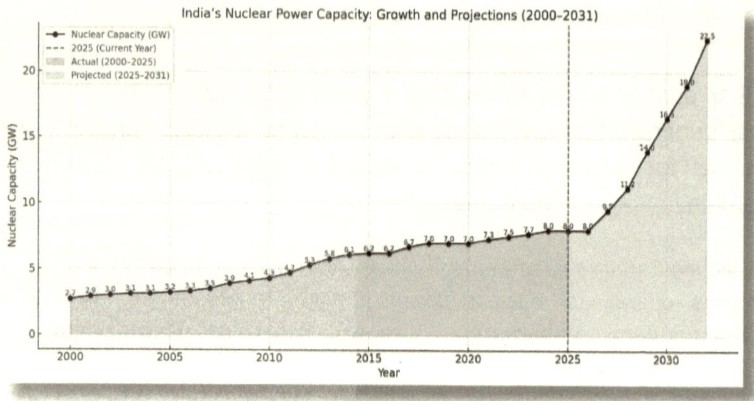

Global Partnerships: Agreements with France (EDF) for EPR reactors and Russia (Rosatom) for VVER reactors are set to accelerate the rollout of next-generation nuclear technology.

Nuclear energy will be vital for ensuring base-load power and mitigating the intermittency challenges of renewable sources like solar and wind. However, public perception, high capital costs, and regulatory hurdles remain challenges to scaling up nuclear power.

The Role of Private Sector and Public-Private Partnerships in Power Generation

The private sector continues to play a pivotal role in India's energy transition, particularly in accelerating renewable energy deployment and modernizing power infrastructure. Public-private partnerships (PPPs) have emerged as vital instruments for scaling up capacity and improving grid resilience.

Private Sector Participation:

- As of March 2025, the private sector controls approximately **48% of India's installed power generation capacity,** up from 47% in 2024.
- Major players such as Adani Green Energy, Tata Power, ReNew Power, and JSW Energy have spearheaded growth in renewable energy projects:

  - **Adani Green Energy:** Surpassed **28 GW of installed renewable capacity** in 2025, with major solar and wind projects in Gujarat and Rajasthan.

  - Tata Power: Expanded its rooftop solar portfolio to over **1.4 GW,** leading the market in distributed energy solutions.

  - ReNew Power: Operates over 14 GW of renewable assets, including India's largest wind-solar hybrid plants.

Public-Private Partnerships (PPPs):

Public-Private Partnerships (PPPs) remain vital for large-scale energy infrastructure development, particularly in renewable energy generation and grid modernization. These collaborations combine public policy support with private investment and technical expertise, enabling India to accelerate its clean energy transition.

Major PPP Projects

- **Rewa Solar Park** (Madhya Pradesh): One of India's largest solar projects, developed under a PPP model, supplies clean electricity to Delhi Metro and other clients.
- **Kutch Wind Project** (Gujarat): A significant PPP venture harnessing the region's strong wind potential for utility-scale power generation.

Green Energy Corridors (GEC): Backbone of Renewable Integration

India's **Green Energy Corridors** (GEC) initiative plays a critical role in integrating renewable energy into the national grid, addressing the variability challenges posed by solar and wind power. These corridors ensure efficient transmission of renewable energy from generation-rich regions to demand centers across the country.

Phase I (2015–2021)

- **Objective:** Facilitate the integration of **33 GW** of renewable energy.

- Focus Areas: Renewable energy-rich states like **Tamil Nadu, Rajasthan, Gujarat, Andhra Pradesh, Karnataka, and Madhya Pradesh**.

- Key Developments:
  - **9,400 circuit kilometers** (ckm) of transmission lines constructed.
  - **19,000 MVA** of substations commissioned.

Phase II (GEC-II)

- **Launched:** Early 2022

- **Goal:** Develop transmission systems for an additional 20 GW of renewable energy capacity, supporting India's ambitious 500 GW renewable target by 2030.

- **Focus Areas:** Expansion into northern and northeastern states, improving renewable energy flow to traditionally underserved regions.

- **Progress (2025):**
  - Over **6,200 ckm** of new transmission lines completed.
  - Significant investments in **high-voltage direct current (HVDC)** systems to handle variable renewable energy.

The Green Energy Corridors exemplify how PPP models can deliver critical infrastructure for India's clean energy future, balancing growth, equity, and sustainability.

As of **March 31, 2025**, India stands at a pivotal juncture in its quest for energy security.

While **coal and other fossil fuels** continue to dominate the power generation landscape, contributing nearly **66% of total electricity output,** the **rapid expansion of renewable energy sources**—particularly solar and wind—signals a decisive shift toward cleaner and more sustainable energy.

The government's support for **public-private partnerships (PPPs)**, along with robust private sector investments, is expected to propel India toward its ambitious **500 GW non-fossil fuel energy target by 2030**, laying the foundation for a secure and sustainable energy future.

Arun: Ankit, I've got to say, this chapter really captures the shift in India's energy landscape. You've done a great job breaking down the power generation mix and giving clear data about each energy source.

Ankit: Thanks, Arun. It's a complicated topic, but I wanted to make it as clear as possible, especially with how coal is still dominant but renewables are catching up fast.

Arun: Yeah, I noticed that. The way you covered the Green Energy Corridors really stood out to me. It's interesting to see how these projects are addressing the challenges of integrating renewables into the grid.

Ankit: Exactly. The infrastructure is key. Without it, renewable energy would just get stuck in bottlenecks, and we'd never hit our targets.

Chapter 4: Renewable Energy Revolution in India

- Solar Energy: India's Ambitions and Achievements

- Wind Energy Potential: Key Projects and Future Roadmaps

- Emerging Technologies: Biomass, Geothermal, and Tidal Energy

- Renewable Energy Policies: National Solar Mission, Green Tariffs, and More

- Financing Renewable Energy: Investments, FDI, and Incentives

Arun: Ankit, for this chapter I feel like we need some fresh insight from someone deep in the renewable energy space—especially with the solar industry. Who do you think we should reach out to?

Ankit: You're right. I've been thinking to include my wife Kamini Gupta. She's the Communication Manager at Axitec Solar—one of the top solar module manufacturers. She has her finger on the pulse of the solar sector, and she's really well-informed about what's happening across the renewable energy space. I think she could give us valuable input for this chapter.

Arun: That's a great idea! Kamini's definitely someone who can add depth to the discussion. Should I draft an email, or are you planning to call her?

Ankit: I'll call her. This is too important for an email—let's get her onboard directly.

Ankit picks up his phone and calls Kamini.

Kamini: Hey Ankit, you know na its my office time...

Ankit: Yes my madamji. Actually, I'm working on a book, and I'm at the point where I need some expert input for the chapter on renewable energy. I was wondering if you'd be willing to help out with this chapter?

Kamini: Of course, I'd love to help! The renewable energy sector is evolving so fast, and it would be great to contribute. What exactly do you need?

Ankit: I'm looking for in-depth information on the current state of India's renewable energy sector—solar, wind, emerging technologies like biomass, and how the policy frameworks are shaping up. If you could provide some insight and share data on the latest trends, that would be perfect.

Kamini: Consider it done. I'll pull together some key details about what's happening in the renewable energy space in India. Give me a few days, and I'll send everything over.

Ankit: That sounds amazing.

Kamini, after a few days compiled what all is required for the book.

You know, India has really placed itself at the forefront of the global energy transition. Over the past decade, we've seen incredible growth in our renewable energy sector. It's not just about keeping up with the world's shift toward sustainable energy—it's about leading it.

India's been setting some ambitious targets, like reducing our reliance on fossil fuels and building a more secure energy future. And we're doing it through a combination of strong government policies, massive private investments, and working with international partners.

What's really exciting is how we're harnessing our natural resources. Solar, wind, and even biomass—they're all playing a big role in this shift. And while solar and wind are leading the way, we're also starting to see technologies like geothermal and tidal energy come into the mix.

These emerging sectors might be small right now, but they're growing and showing a lot of promise for the future.

But it's not just about the technology—it's the policy frameworks that have really made this happen. Programs like the National Solar Mission, green tariffs, and the Production-Linked Incentive (PLI) scheme have been game changers. They've given the renewable energy sector the support it needs to grow quickly and attract both domestic and foreign investments.

By March 2024, we've already hit some impressive milestones in solar and wind energy. India's renewable energy capacity is on track to meet our goal of 500 GW by 2030. It's a bold target, but everything we've been doing so far shows that we're well on our way.

This chapter gives you a clear picture of how all these elements—technology, policy, investment—are coming together to shape India's energy future. We're not just participating in the global renewable energy revolution—we're helping lead it.

India is at the forefront of a renewable energy revolution, reshaping its power landscape to meet the twin challenges of **energy security** and **climate change mitigation**.

Over the past decade, the country has emerged as one of the fastest-growing renewable energy markets in the world, driven by ambitious targets, robust policy frameworks, and a surge in private and public investments.

As of **March 2025**, renewable energy sources account for nearly **37% of India's total installed capacity**, with solar and wind power leading this transition. The government's commitment to achieving 500 GW of non-fossil fuel capacity by 2030 underscores the centrality of renewables in India's energy future.

This chapter explores India's renewable energy journey in detail—highlighting key technologies like solar, wind, biomass, geothermal, and tidal energy, analyzing policy interventions, and assessing the financial ecosystem that supports this growth. It provides insights into how India is navigating the challenges of scaling up clean energy while ensuring equitable access and economic development.

As the country charts its path toward a net-zero future, renewables are no longer an alternative—they are the foundation of India's 21st-century energy architecture.

Solar Energy: India's Ambitions and Achievements

India has emerged as a global leader in solar energy, transforming its position from an energy-deficient nation to a hub for clean power generation. Solar energy lies at the heart of India's renewable energy strategy, driven by abundant sunlight, ambitious targets, and falling technology costs.

Installed Capacity (March 2025)

- As of **March 31, 2025**, India's installed solar capacity reached **90 GW**, up from **67 GW in 2023**, marking an average annual addition of nearly 11 GW in recent years.

- Solar now accounts for **19.9% of India's total power generation** capacity and nearly 54% of total renewable energy capacity.

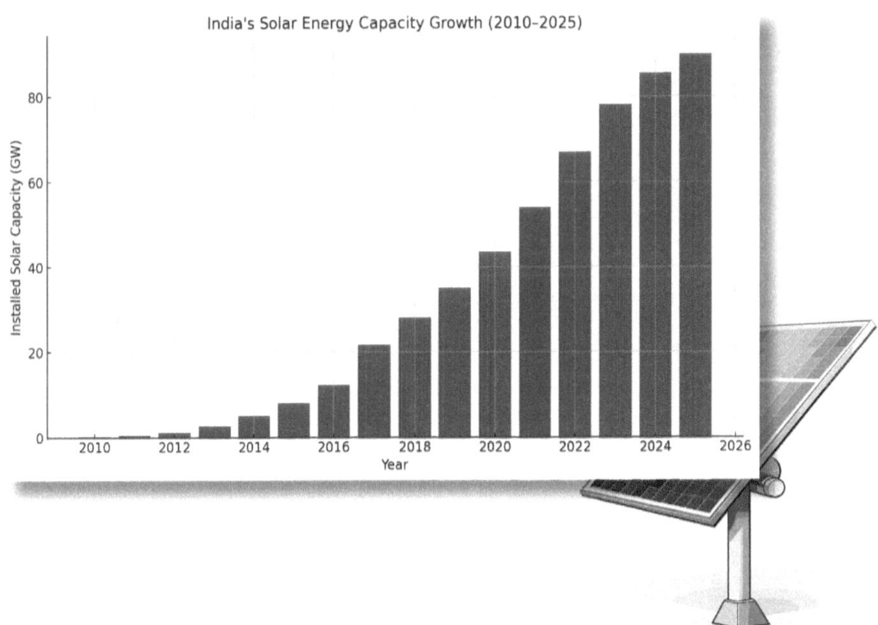

Key Solar Achievements:

- **Bhadla Solar Park (Rajasthan):** World's largest solar park with 2.25 GW capacity.

- **Pavagada Solar Park (Karnataka):** Generates over 2 GW, meeting a significant share of Karnataka's electricity demand.

- **Residential Rooftop Solar:** Adoption accelerated through government subsidies and net metering policies, crossing 8 GW rooftop installations nationwide.

- **International Solar Alliance (ISA):** India, as a founding member, has emerged as a global solar diplomacy leader, fostering cooperation with over 120 countries.

Ambitions and Future Targets

- India targets **280 GW of solar capacity by 2030**, forming over 50% of its 500 GW non-fossil fuel energy goal.

- Solar Manufacturing Push: Under the Production Linked Incentive (PLI) Scheme, domestic solar module manufacturing capacity is set to exceed **50 GW per annum by 2026**.

- Focus areas for 2025–2030 include:
    - Floating Solar Projects on reservoirs and dams.
    - Scaling up agro-photovoltaics to combine agriculture with solar power.
    - Solar-wind hybrid projects to optimize land and grid usage.

Wind Energy Potential: Key Projects and Future Roadmaps

India is the world's fourth-largest wind power producer, with vast potential across its long coastline and central plains. Wind energy continues to play a crucial role in the country's renewable energy mix, complementing solar power and ensuring a diversified clean energy portfolio.

Wind Energy Potential:

India's long coastline, especially in states like **Tamil Nadu, Gujarat, and Karnataka**, offers excellent wind energy potential. The country has identified over **300 GW of wind power potential**, with onshore projects leading the way in harnessing this resource.

The **National Institute of Wind Energy (NIWE)** has conducted updated studies showing that regions like Tamil Nadu, Gujarat, and Maharashtra hold some of the highest potential for onshore wind generation due to favorable wind speeds and supportive state policies.

Key Wind Energy Projects

- Muppandal Wind Farm (Tamil Nadu): The largest onshore wind farm in India, with an installed capacity of **1.5 GW as of March 2025**. Favorable wind conditions and consistent state support make Tamil Nadu a national leader in wind energy generation.

- Kutch Wind Project (Gujarat): One of the largest wind projects in western India, with over **1.2 GW of installed capacity**, this project plays a key role in Gujarat's growing renewable energy portfolio and contributes to the Green Energy Corridor transmission network.

Offshore Wind Development

Offshore wind is an emerging frontier in India's wind energy sector.
- The first offshore wind project, planned off the coast of **Gujarat**, aims to add **1 GW of capacity by 2027**.
- India's offshore wind potential is estimated at **70 GW** along its western and southern coastlines.
- The government's roadmap targets **5 GW of offshore wind capacity by 2030**, with pilot projects underway near Tamil Nadu and Gujarat.

Future Roadmap:

India aims to reach **140 GW of wind capacity by 2030**, with significant focus on both onshore and offshore projects.

Wind energy prices in India remain highly competitive, with recent auction bids dropping to **₹2.3–2.5/kWh (USD 0.028–0.03)** in 2024-25, making it one of the most affordable renewable energy sources globally.

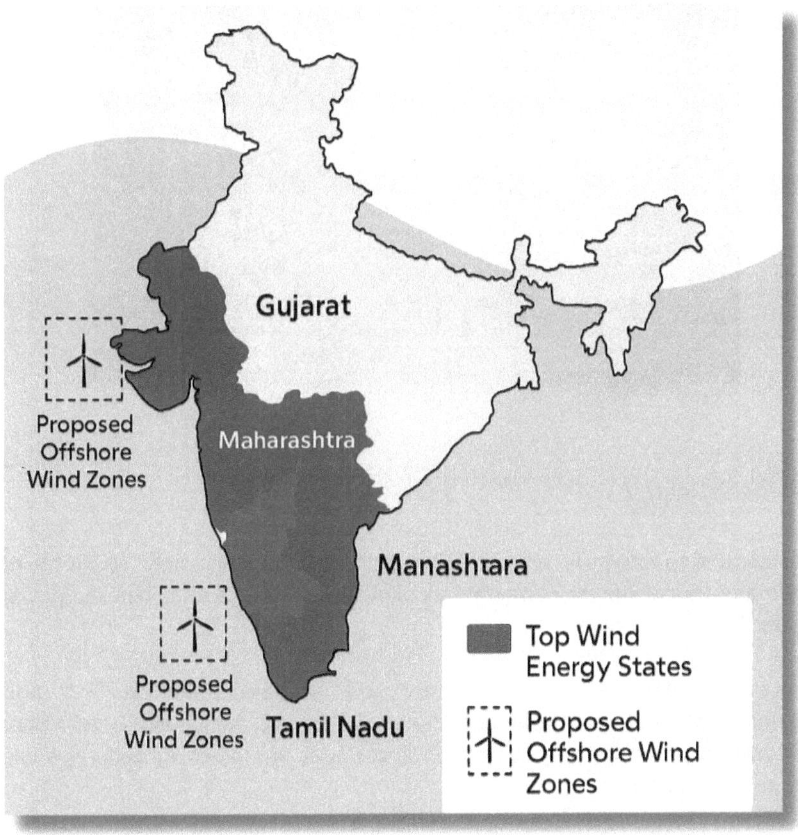

Emerging Technologies: Biomass, Geothermal, and Tidal Energy

While solar and wind dominate India's renewable energy landscape, emerging technologies like biomass, geothermal, and tidal energy are beginning to gain attention as the country diversifies its clean energy portfolio.

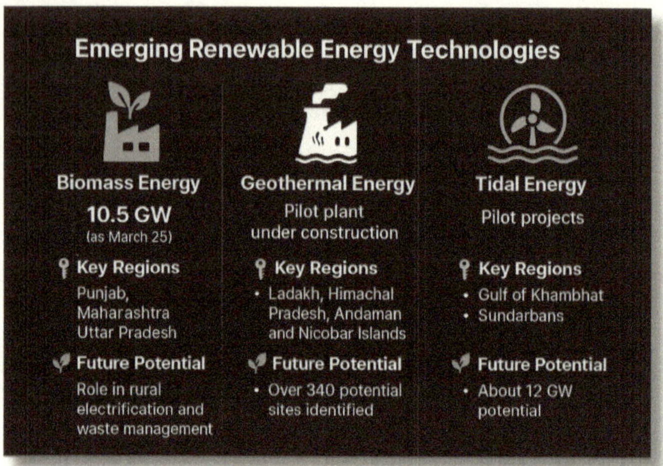

Biomass Energy:

Installed Capacity: By **March 2025**, India had approximately **10.5 GW of biomass-based power capacity**, accounting for 2.3% of total installed power capacity.

Biomass energy plays a significant role in **rural electrification and agricultural waste management**. States like Punjab, Maharashtra, and Uttar Pradesh have led the way in using crop residues and other agricultural waste for power generation.

The government actively promotes **co-generation in industries** such as sugar and paper, where excess biomass is used to produce electricity and thermal energy for internal consumption and grid supply.

Geothermal Energy:

Although still in its infancy, geothermal energy holds promise for India's future energy mix.

- **Pilot Projects:** The **first geothermal power plant in India**, planned in **Puga Valley (Ladakh)**, is expected to generate **200 kW of power** and is currently under construction as of early 2025.

- **Potential Sites:** The Geological Survey of India (GSI) has identified over **340 geothermal sites across the country**, with high potential in Ladakh, Himachal Pradesh, and the Andaman & Nicobar Islands.

- **International Partnerships:** India is exploring collaborations with countries like Iceland and Kenya, leveraging their experience in geothermal technology and operations.

Tidal Energy:

India has significant untapped potential for tidal energy, particularly in regions like the **Gulf of Khambhat (Gujarat)** and the **Sundarbans (West Bengal)**.
- Estimated Potential: Around **12 GW of tidal energy potential** has been identified across India's coastline.

- Pilot Projects: The **first tidal energy pilot projects are under development,** but high upfront costs and technological challenges have slowed large-scale deployment.

- Focus is shifting toward **hybrid ocean energy** systems that combine tidal and wave energy for greater efficiency.

Renewable Energy Policies: National Solar Mission, Green Tariffs, and More

India's renewable energy revolution is underpinned by robust policy frameworks and proactive government initiatives that have catalyzed rapid growth in the sector. These policies not only drive domestic deployment but also position India as a global leader in clean energy innovation and collaboration.

National Solar Mission (NSM):

Launched in 2010, the Jawaharlal Nehru National Solar Mission (NSM) remains the backbone of India's solar expansion.

- **Initial Target:** Achieve 100 GW of solar capacity by 2022.

- **Updated Target (2030):** Now extended to **280 GW of solar capacity** as part of India's 500 GW renewable energy goal.

- Achievements:
    - Development of mega solar parks like **Bhadla (Rajasthan)** and **Pavagada (Karnataka).**

    - Rapid growth of **off-grid solar applications** and **rooftop installations**, which reached **8 GW as of March 2025**.

Renewable Purchase Obligations (RPOs)

RPOs mandate that distribution companies (DISCOMs) and large electricity consumers source a certain percentage of their energy from renewable sources.

- **2025 RPO Targets:** Require **24% of electricity consumption** to be sourced from renewables, up from **21% in 2024**.

- Several states, including **Gujarat and Maharashtra**, have overachieved their RPO targets due to large-scale renewable energy deployments.

Green Tariffs

To encourage industries and businesses to shift to renewable energy, several states have introduced **green tariffs**.

- These tariffs allow consumers to pay a premium to ensure their electricity comes exclusively from renewable sources.

- 2025 Rates:
  - Karnataka: ₹4.4/kWh
  - Gujarat: ₹4.3/kWh
  - Maharashtra: ₹4.5/kWh

Production-Linked Incentive (PLI) Scheme

The PLI scheme provides financial incentives to manufacturers of solar modules, batteries, and other renewable energy components.

- **Objective:** Boost **domestic manufacturing capacity** and reduce dependence on imports, particularly from China.

- **Impact:** By 2025, India's solar module manufacturing capacity crossed **45 GW per annum**, with new facilities set up in Gujarat, Tamil Nadu, and Uttar Pradesh.

International Solar Alliance (ISA)

Launched in 2015 by India and France, the ISA has become a major platform for promoting global clean energy cooperation.

Key Initiatives: Mobilization of $2 billion in funding for solar projects in Africa and Asia, and support for solar mini-grids in remote regions.

Financing Renewable Energy: Investments, FDI, and Incentives

India's renewable energy sector continues to attract significant domestic and international investments, underpinned by supportive policies, innovative financing mechanisms, and strong market potential.

Investment Trends:

- Total investments in India's renewable energy sector from **2014 to 2025** exceeded **USD 115 billion**, reflecting the country's emergence as a global clean energy hub.

- **2024-25 Investment Record:** India's renewable energy sector attracted an all-time high of **USD 17.2 billion**, driven largely by mega solar parks, wind projects, and energy storage initiatives.

- Major global firms and investment funds such as **BlackRock, Brookfield, and SoftBank** have deepened their commitments to India's renewable projects.

Foreign Direct Investment (FDI)

- FDI inflows into India's renewable energy sector have grown steadily, surpassing **USD 12.5 billion between 2018 and 2025**.

- The Indian government's policy allowing **100% FDI under the automatic route** for renewable energy projects has facilitated seamless international capital flows to domestic developers.

Incentives and Subsidies

The government has introduced multiple financial incentives to drive renewable energy adoption:

Accelerated Depreciation: Allows companies to claim accelerated depreciation on renewable energy investments, reducing tax burdens.

Viability Gap Funding (VGF): Bridges the gap between project costs and market tariffs for large-scale solar and wind projects.

Renewable Energy Certificates (RECs): Tradable certificates incentivizing renewable energy production and helping entities meet Renewable Purchase Obligation (RPO) targets.

Green Bonds

- Green bonds have emerged as a major tool to finance renewable energy projects in India.

- As of **March 2025**, Indian companies raised over **USD 8.3 billion** through green bonds.

- Both public sector entities like **NTPC** and private players like **ReNew Power** and **Adani Green Energy** have been key issuers.

As of March 2025, India's renewable energy journey stands as a testament to its commitment to sustainability, energy security, and global climate leadership.

With solar and wind energy forming the backbone of this transformation, and emerging technologies like biomass, geothermal, and tidal energy adding diversity, the nation is rapidly moving toward its 500 GW non-fossil fuel target by 2030.

Government policies, innovative financing mechanisms, and active private sector participation have created a vibrant ecosystem for clean energy growth. However, to fully realize this potential, India must address challenges such as grid integration, storage solutions, and equitable access.

The renewable energy revolution is no longer a distant vision—it is the foundation of India's future as a global leader in sustainable development.

Arun: Ankit, I have to say, Kamini really knows her stuff. The way she explained the renewable energy transition was spot-on. She didn't just provide facts—she brought it to life.

Ankit: Exactly. The way she broke down everything—from solar and wind to the emerging technologies like biomass and tidal energy—it felt like we were getting the inside story of India's energy revolution. And the policy angle she highlighted was really key.

Arun: Yeah, it was interesting to see how those government initiatives like the National Solar Mission and the PLI scheme are driving all of this growth. I knew about the big projects like Bhadla and Kurnool, but she gave us a real understanding of the policies behind them.

Ankit: That's what I loved about her input. She didn't just give us technical data; she connected the dots between policy, investments, and on-the-ground progress. It's no wonder India is becoming such a leader in renewable energy.

Arun: I also didn't realize how quickly solar and wind have become major players in the energy mix. 80 GW of solar and 47 GW of wind already? And we're aiming for 500 GW of renewable capacity by 2030? That's massive.

Ankit: Yeah, it's no small feat. And I'm really glad Kamini touched on the challenges too—like the grid integration issues and land acquisition problems. We're making great progress, but it's clear we still have hurdles to overcome.

Arun: True. But what really stood out to me was the role of the private sector. She talked about the big players like Axitec, but also how the foreign direct investment and incentives like accelerated depreciation are attracting global interest.

Ankit: Exactly. It's one thing to have ambitious goals, but the financial side is just as critical. The fact that India's attracted over USD 100 billion in renewable energy investments speaks volumes.

Arun: Kamini's insights really made the chapter feel comprehensive. It's not just about solar panels or wind farms—it's about the entire ecosystem, from policies to financing to international partnerships.

Ankit: I'm glad we reached out to her. Her perspective made this chapter so much stronger, and I think anyone reading it will come away with a deeper understanding of where India is headed.

Arun: No doubt about it. This chapter has really set the tone for what's possible in India's renewable energy future. I think we've nailed it.

Ankit: Agreed. I'm going to send Kamini a thank-you note for her contributions. She really helped bring this chapter to life.

Arun: Definitely. Now that we've wrapped this one up, let's see where we can bring in more experts like her for the next chapters.

Ankit: Good plan. On to the next one.

Chapter 5: Power Transmission and Storage: The Missing Link

- India's National Grid: Strengths and Weaknesses

- Energy Storage Technologies: Batteries, Pumped Storage, and Beyond

- Smart Grids and Microgrids: Modernizing Power Transmission

- Energy Banking: Unlocking Grid Flexibility in India

- Power Transmission Losses and Efficiency Challenges

- The Role of Cross-Border Electricity Trade in India's Energy Security

While India has made remarkable strides in power generation—especially in renewable energy—the quest for energy security remains incomplete without addressing the critical areas of power transmission and storage.

As renewable energy sources like solar and wind become an increasingly dominant part of India's energy mix, they bring unique challenges of intermittency and grid integration.

The efficiency, resilience, and modernization of India's power grid are essential to ensuring a reliable and consistent electricity supply, particularly as peak demand crossed 260 GW in 2025, straining existing infrastructure.

This chapter examines the strengths and weaknesses of India's national grid, highlighting its ability to support growing energy demand while identifying bottlenecks that hinder its efficiency.

It also explores the transformative potential of emerging energy storage technologies—battery systems, pumped hydro storage, and green hydrogen—which are crucial for managing the variability of renewables and enabling India's clean energy ambitions.

Furthermore, the chapter discusses the importance of modernizing the grid through smart grids and microgrids, technologies that can optimize electricity flows in real time and reduce transmission losses.

India's ambitious energy transition demands more than just generating renewable power; it requires a comprehensive overhaul of how that power is transmitted, stored, and distributed. Solving these challenges is the vital missing link in building a cleaner, smarter, and more secure energy future.

India's National Grid: Strengths and Weaknesses

India's national grid is one of the **largest and most complex power grids** in the world, with a total transmission capacity of **470 GW as of March 31, 2025**.

Managed by the **Power Grid Corporation of India Ltd. (PGCIL)**, the national grid connects the entire country, integrating all five regional grids: **Northern, Southern, Eastern, Western, and Northeastern**.

Strengths:

- **Unified National Grid:** Since the successful integration of regional grids in 2013, India operates a single synchronous grid, enabling seamless electricity flow across regions and facilitating power trading through market platforms.

- **High Transmission Capacity:** The transmission system has been strengthened significantly and now handles **peak loads exceeding 250 GW (recorded in July 2025)** without major disruptions, reflecting improved grid resilience.

- **Green Energy Corridors (GEC):**
  - A critical initiative to integrate renewable energy into the grid, **GEC Phase I** completed 9,800 circuit kilometers (ckm) of transmission lines and **20,000 MVA** of substation capacity by early 2025.

  - **GEC Phase II,** launched in 2022, is underway to add an additional 10,500 ckm of transmission lines and support **20 GW of new renewable energy capacity.**

  - Key renewable-rich states like Rajasthan, Tamil Nadu, and Gujarat now export excess renewable energy to deficit regions.

Weaknesses:

Transmission Bottlenecks:
- Despite grid expansion, remote regions (especially in the Northeast and some parts of Ladakh and Andaman & Nicobar Islands) face bottlenecks due to inadequate transmission infrastructure, leading to grid instability and frequent supply disruptions.

Capacity Constraints for Renewables:
- The grid is struggling to handle the intermittent nature of renewable energy. States with high renewable penetration like Gujarat and Tamil Nadu face grid congestion during peak solar and wind generation hours, necessitating curtailment of renewable energy output.

Financial Stress on Distribution Companies (DISCOMs):
- While transmission infrastructure has improved, financially stressed DISCOMs hamper overall grid efficiency. Many lack resources to invest in last-mile upgrades, causing technical losses and billing inefficiencies.

Energy Storage Technologies: Batteries, Pumped Storage, and Beyond

Energy storage lies at the heart of India's clean energy transition, offering critical solutions to the intermittency challenges of solar and wind power. As renewable energy continues to expand rapidly, robust storage systems are essential to ensure grid stability, manage peak demand, and enable round-the-clock clean energy supply.

As of March 31, 2025, India's installed energy storage capacity remains in the early stages, but significant progress is being made across battery storage, pumped hydro, and emerging technologies.

Battery energy storage systems (BESS) have witnessed rapid growth in recent years. India's **grid-connected battery storage capacity** has risen to **3.8 GW/8.2 GWh in 2025**, a notable increase from **2.5 GW/5 GWh in 2024.**

Large-scale projects are leading the way. The **Kurnool Ultra Mega Solar Park** (Andhra Pradesh) now **houses India's largest battery energy storage system**, with a capacity of 350 MW/700 MWh.

Similarly, the **Delhi-NCR BESS pilot project**, with **100 MW/200 MWh capacity**, is designed to provide grid stabilization and peak shaving solutions for urban regions.

Currently, lithium-ion batteries dominate the storage landscape, but significant research and pilot deployments are underway for alternative technologies such as sodium-ion, flow batteries, and solid-state batteries to improve efficiency and reduce costs.

Pumped hydro storage remains the most mature and cost-effective form of large-scale energy storage in India.

The country's operational pumped **hydro capacity has grown to 5.2 GW** as of March 2025.

New projects, including the **1 GW Tehri Dam Pumped Storage Plant** (Uttarakhand) and the **1.44 GW Pench Pumped Storage Project** (Madhya Pradesh), are under construction and expected to be operational by 2026.

With an estimated **potential exceeding 96 GW**, pumped hydro could play a pivotal role in stabilizing India's renewable energy integration efforts.

Emerging storage technologies are also beginning to gain traction. **Compressed Air Energy Storage (CAES)** pilot projects in Rajasthan and Gujarat are exploring scalable, long-duration storage solutions.

Meanwhile, green hydrogen storage is being aggressively developed under the **National Green Hydrogen Mission**, launched in 2023.

Green hydrogen is emerging as a dual-purpose solution—serving as an energy storage medium and a clean fuel for transportation, heavy industries, and power-to-gas systems.

Smart Grids and Microgrids: Modernizing Power Transmission

Modernizing India's power grid is essential for improving efficiency, integrating renewable energy, and reducing transmission and distribution losses. Smart grids and microgrids are critical components of this transformation, enabling India to move toward a more flexible, resilient, and consumer-centric energy system.

Power Grid India Corporation Limited

Smart Grids:

A smart grid uses digital technology to monitor and manage electricity flows in real time, allowing for dynamic adjustments to supply and demand. This reduces losses, optimizes renewable integration, and empowers consumers to make informed energy choices.

- **National Smart Grid Mission (NSGM):** Launched in 2015, this mission aims to modernize India's grid by integrating smart meters, demand response systems, and automation technologies.

- **Smart Meter Rollout:** By March 2025, India has installed **34 million smart meters**, with a target to reach 250 million by 2026.

  - Impact: Smart meters have reduced distribution losses by **15–20%** in pilot states and enabled time-of-use tariffs, encouraging consumers to shift usage to off-peak hours.

Microgrids:

A microgrid is a localized energy system that can operate independently or in coordination with the national grid. Microgrids are especially valuable in rural and remote areas where grid connectivity is unreliable or absent.

- **Current Deployment:** By March 2025, India has developed over 750 MW of microgrid capacity, primarily in rural regions and islands.

- Key Initiatives:
  - The **Remote Village Electrification Program** has accelerated microgrid development in **off-grid** areas, providing clean and reliable electricity to underserved communities.

  - In the **Sundarbans**, a solar-battery microgrid powers thousands of households, replacing diesel generators and reducing carbon emissions.

Image Credit: Canary Media

Energy Banking: Unlocking Grid Flexibility in India

Energy banking is emerging as a vital tool in India's energy transition, offering flexibility for renewable energy integration and supporting grid stability.

Much like financial banking, energy banking allows renewable energy producers—particularly those operating under open access systems—to "deposit" surplus energy into the grid during periods of overproduction, such as when the sun shines brightest or the wind blows strongest.

Later, during high-demand periods or when renewable generation dips, producers can "withdraw" this stored energy to meet their needs or supply consumers.

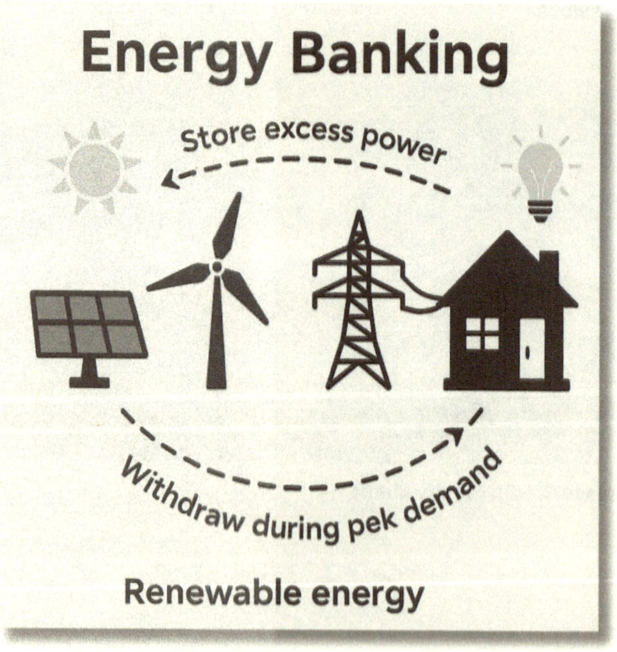

Grid-Level Energy Banking Policies for Open Access

India's regulatory framework for energy banking has evolved significantly in recent years, driven by the growing presence of **open access consumers** who procure renewable energy directly from producers instead of relying solely on distribution companies **(DISCOMs)**.

The **Ministry of Power** and various **State Electricity Regulatory Commissions (SERCs)** have introduced policies that enable seamless exchange of energy under open access, making energy banking an effective mechanism to manage renewable energy variability.

Key Features of Energy Banking Policies:

- Open Access Provision: Under India's Open Access framework, industries and large consumers can procure renewable energy directly from producers. Energy banking helps them balance supply and demand fluctuations, particularly in renewable-heavy portfolios.

- State-Level Energy Banking Policies: Progressive states such as Karnataka, Rajasthan, Tamil Nadu, and Gujarat have implemented energy banking frameworks that allow producers to store surplus energy and withdraw it during peak demand, reducing curtailment and improving renewable utilization.

Energy Banking Charges and Policies by State

Each state in India has implemented its own version of energy banking policies, with varying levels of banking charges and conditions. Here's an overview of some prominent state-level policies:

Here's an overview of some prominent state-level policies:

State	Banking Period	Banking Charges	State Support
Karnataka	Monthly/Annual	5% + wheeling & transmission	Supports renewable integration with open access banking.
Tamil Nadu	Up to 6 months	12% (off-peak withdrawals only)	Encourages grid utilization; limited to off-peak withdrawals.
Rajasthan	Monthly	10%	Facilitates solar and wind banking under open access.
Madhya Pradesh	Monthly	2% (lowest in India)	Lowest charges promote renewable investment.
Gujarat	Monthly	8% of banked energy	Promotes solar-wind hybrid energy banking.
Andhra Pradesh	Up to 1 month	6% + transmission losses	Focus on industrial consumers and renewable surplus management.
Maharashtra	Monthly	9% + wheeling charges	Supports banking with added wheeling charges for renewables.
Punjab	Monthly	7%	Promotes rural microgrid renewable banking and flexibility.

Power Transmission Losses and Efficiency Challenges

India's **transmission and distribution (T&D)** losses have long been a persistent challenge, affecting the efficiency, reliability, and financial viability of its power sector. Despite notable improvements over the past decade, T&D losses in India remain significantly higher than global best practices.

As of **March 2025**, the national average for T&D losses stands at **16.2%**, a marginal reduction from 17% in March 2024. However, this is still nearly double the levels seen in advanced economies, where T&D losses are typically in the range of 6–8%.

Causes of High Losses:

- Technical Losses:
    - These losses occur due to inherent resistance in transmission lines and electrical equipment. India's vast geography, coupled with the long distances over which electricity is transmitted—from renewable-rich states like **Rajasthan and Tamil Nadu** to industrial hubs—exacerbates technical losses. Aging infrastructure and under-capacity transmission networks further contribute to inefficiencies.

- Non-Technical Losses:
    - Non-technical losses primarily stem from **power theft**, **billing inefficiencies**, and **unmetered connections**.
    - States such as Uttar Pradesh and Bihar continue to report some of the highest levels of non-technical losses in the country, with theft and faulty metering systems undermining distribution companies' financial health.

The Role of Cross-Border Electricity Trade in India's Energy Security

India's energy security strategy increasingly recognizes the importance of **cross-border electricity trade (CBET)** with neighboring countries. By leveraging its geographical position and grid infrastructure, India aims to transform the **South Asian region** into an interconnected electricity market that supports **energy security**, **grid stability**, and **renewable energy integration**.

Current Cross-Border Trade:

India is already a net exporter of electricity to its neighbors, with over 6,100 MW of cross-border transmission capacity as of March 2025. These interconnections strengthen regional cooperation and provide economic and technical benefits to all participating countries.

Nepal: India imports **hydroelectricity** from Nepal during the wet season and exports electricity during dry seasons to help Nepal balance its grid. As of 2025, India and Nepal share over **2,400 MW of electricity trade capacity**, enabled by upgraded transmission lines like the **Dhalkebar-Muzaffarpur** line.

Bhutan: India imports around **2,000 MW of hydropower** from Bhutan, primarily from projects like the **Tala, Chhukha**, and **Mangdechhu** dams. These imports are critical during the monsoon season when Bhutan's hydro generation peaks, allowing India to meet rising demand while supporting Bhutan's economy through electricity exports.

Bangladesh: India exports approximately **1,250 MW of electricity** to Bangladesh, contributing significantly to the country's growing power needs. New transmission lines under development, such as the Tripura-Comilla interconnection, are expected to increase bilateral trade capacity to 1,800 MW by 2026.

India is actively working to enhance its cross-border electricity trade network and strengthen regional energy security through new infrastructure and partnerships.

- **India–Sri Lanka Undersea Power Link:**
  - Plans are underway for the **India–Sri Lanka undersea power transmission link**, which is expected to facilitate up to **1,200 MW of cross-border electricity trade**. This strategic interconnection will enable Sri Lanka to access surplus renewable energy from India and contribute to regional grid stability.

- Potential India–Myanmar Partnerships:
  - India is exploring opportunities to partner with **Myanmar** for electricity trade. Given Myanmar's significant **hydropower and solar potential**, such a collaboration could support Myanmar's electrification goals while enhancing energy cooperation in the region.

South Asian Power Pool:

To further deepen energy integration, there are ongoing discussions to establish a **South Asian Regional Power Pool**. This initiative aims to create a unified electricity market across **India, Nepal, Bhutan, Bangladesh**, and **Sri Lanka**.

- A regional power pool would allow member countries to **share electricity resources efficiently**, reducing the need for excess generation capacity in individual nations.
- It would also improve grid resilience, support renewable energy integration, and lower costs through regional optimization of supply and demand.

Arun: Ankit, I think we've covered a lot of ground here with the transmission and storage aspects, but there's something missing.

Ankit: Really? What do you think we're missing?

Arun: Well, you've laid out the challenges and strengths of India's national grid and energy storage very clearly. But when we talk about power transmission and the integration of renewables, shouldn't we also highlight the key players—the DISCOMs, power operators, and companies working in the microgrid space? We mention the overall infrastructure, but what about the people and companies actually running the show?

Ankit: Good point. I did focus heavily on the technology and infrastructure, but you're right. We didn't name any of the DISCOMs or companies that are pivotal in making this work.

Arun: Exactly. For example, Power Grid Corporation of India (PGCIL) manages the entire national grid, right? But then there are the distribution companies like MSEDCL, Tata Power, and Adani Electricity in Mumbai that play a critical role in getting power to consumers. And for microgrids, companies like Boond Solar, Husk Power Systems, and Oorja Development Solutions are doing some incredible work in rural areas.

Ankit: Yeah, you're absolutely right. The chapter feels incomplete without giving credit to the people and companies who are actually driving the system forward. And let's not forget the smart grid solutions providers like Schneider Electric and Siemens, who are at the forefront of modernizing our grid.

Arun: Exactly. It's not just about the infrastructure or the numbers—it's about who's making all of this happen. Readers need to see who the big players are and understand their impact.

Ankit: I can't believe I overlooked that. I'll definitely add sections that highlight the key DISCOMs, power operators, and microgrid companies. I think it will make the chapter much more complete.

Arun: It'll definitely add more context. Plus, mentioning the innovative companies like Husk Power Systems and Boond Solar shows how India's solving problems at the grassroots level. It'll give readers a better sense of how broad the effort really is.

Ankit: And it makes the chapter feel more connected. I'll include the names of the big players, especially the distribution companies that are struggling and succeeding. And adding the microgrid companies will also tie in well with the rural electrification efforts we talked about earlier.

Arun: Exactly. This way, it's not just a technical overview—it's a more comprehensive look at the whole system and the people driving it.

Ankit: Thanks for pointing it out, Arun. I'll make the edits and add those details. This chapter is about making sure we see the entire picture—not just the big challenges, but the companies and people addressing them.

Key Players in Power Transmission and Distribution

India's power transmission and distribution ecosystem is anchored by a mix of **public and private sector** players, whose contributions are critical for modernizing the grid and ensuring efficient delivery of electricity across the country. The sector's progress depends heavily on their **financial health, infrastructure investments**, and adoption of **advanced technologies**.

The **Power Grid Corporation of India Ltd. (PGCIL)** continues to be the backbone of the national transmission network. Managing one of the **largest and most complex grids in the world**, PGCIL has expanded its transmission network to over **180,000 circuit kilometers (ckm)** of lines and **450+ substations** by March 2025. Its role in integrating renewable energy into the grid, particularly through initiatives like the **Green Energy Corridors**, has been instrumental in supporting India's clean energy ambitions.

On the distribution side, **Distribution Companies (DISCOMs)** such as **MSEDCL (Maharashtra State Electricity Distribution Company Ltd.)**, **GUVNL (Gujarat Urja Vikas Nigam Ltd.)**, and **TPDDL (Tata Power Delhi Distribution Ltd.)** remain crucial for delivering power to end consumers. However, many DISCOMs, particularly in states like **Uttar Pradesh** and **Bihar**, continue to face challenges of **financial stress, high technical and commercial losses**, and billing inefficiencies.

The **private** sector has stepped in to improve distribution efficiency in several urban centers. Companies like **Tata Power** and **Adani Power** are leveraging advanced metering, automation, and grid management systems to enhance operational performance, reduce losses, and improve service quality.

Microgrids and Decentralized Solutions

Decentralized energy systems, particularly **microgrids**, are emerging as vital solutions for providing **reliable electricity access in rural and remote areas**. These systems enable energy independence in regions where grid connectivity is weak or non-existent.

- **Boond Solar** has implemented numerous **solar microgrids** in off-grid regions, empowering communities previously dependent on expensive and polluting diesel generators.

- **Husk Power Systems** utilizes **hybrid microgrids**, combining **solar and biomass**, to provide 24/7 power to rural villages while supporting productive economic activities.

- **Oorja Development Solutions** focuses on **agro-centric microgrids**, delivering affordable and sustainable power for agricultural irrigation and small-scale processing units.

Together, these companies are demonstrating how innovation in decentralized energy systems can complement large-scale transmission infrastructure and play a key role in achieving universal energy access.

India's power transmission and storage infrastructure remains the backbone of its energy security strategy and the key enabler of its renewable energy transition.

As the country scales up its renewable capacity toward the ambitious 500 GW non-fossil fuel target by 2030, the grid must evolve to meet the challenges of intermittency, rising demand, and regional disparities.

The modernization of the grid through smart technologies, expansion of Green Energy Corridors, reduction of transmission and distribution losses, and deployment of advanced energy storage systems such as batteries, pumped hydro, and green hydrogen will be critical.

Together, these advancements will ensure that India can seamlessly integrate large-scale renewables, empower consumers, and deliver reliable, affordable, and sustainable electricity across the country.

Arun: Alright, now this is looking solid, Ankit. You've really brought in the depth that was missing before. Adding the key players in power transmission and distribution makes it feel more grounded.

Ankit: Yeah, after our last conversation, I realized we can't just talk about the infrastructure without mentioning who's actually running it. Companies like PGCIL, Tata Power, and the DISCOMs are really shaping the power landscape. They're not just names—they're the ones dealing with all the real-world challenges.

Arun: Exactly. It's one thing to discuss transmission systems, but without giving readers an understanding of who's responsible for maintaining and modernizing them, it feels abstract. I think mentioning the financial struggles of DISCOMs like MSEDCL and GUVNL is crucial too. It shows the complexity—how even with infrastructure, money issues can cause delays or inefficiencies.

Ankit: That was my thinking. It's easy to focus on the technology, but the financial health of these entities is just as important. If they can't upgrade infrastructure or handle maintenance, it doesn't matter how advanced the grid is.

Arun: Exactly. And the section on microgrids? That really makes a difference. Highlighting companies like Boond Solar and Husk Power Systems gives the chapter a more forward-looking angle. It shows how the future of energy distribution isn't just in big centralized grids, but in localized, decentralized systems.

Ankit: I wanted to emphasize that. While large-scale grids are necessary, the future in rural and remote areas lies in microgrids. Companies like Boond and Husk Power are doing fantastic work, especially in places where traditional grid infrastructure struggles to reach. It's part of India's broader energy strategy—making sure even the most isolated communities have access to reliable power.

Arun: And that's exactly what gives this chapter its punch. It's not just talking about the present but giving readers a view into the future of decentralized energy. You're showing how India is balancing the national grid with innovative, smaller-scale solutions. Plus, with the examples of solar microgrids providing reliable energy to off-grid communities, it highlights how we're moving towards cleaner, more sustainable energy.

Ankit: Yeah, it really rounds out the chapter. The conversation isn't just about the traditional grid—it's about how we can innovate and push the boundaries with technology like hybrid microgrids.

Arun: And don't forget, mentioning Oorja Development Solutions and others helps readers realize there's a whole sector emerging around these localized energy systems. It's not just theoretical—it's happening right now. People in the industry will appreciate those details.

Ankit: That's true. It's about making this book relevant for professionals who want to know who's making a difference on the ground. It's more than just the tech—it's about the companies and innovators driving that change.

Arun: Exactly. Now with these additions, I feel like the chapter's complete. You've got the big picture of India's national grid, but also the cutting-edge microgrid solutions. It's the perfect mix of the established and the emerging.

Ankit: Thanks, Arun. Your suggestions really helped. I'm glad we added these sections. It makes the chapter more comprehensive and gives it the depth it needed.

Arun: Well, that's what teamwork's about. Now, this chapter has everything—data, real-world examples, and future-facing ideas. It's looking good!

Chapter 6: Battery Energy Storage Systems (BESS) and Their Role in India's Energy Future

- Current Landscape of BESS in India

- Technological Advances in Battery Storage

- Grid-Scale Applications: Integrating Renewables with Storage

- Emerging Business Models: EaaS, P2P Trading, and Distributed Storage

- Battery Recycling and Circular Economy Opportunities

- Policy Landscape and Financial Innovations Supporting BESS

- India vs Global Leaders in Energy Storage: A Comparative Analysis

Ankit: [Looking through his notes] This topic of Battery Energy Storage Systems (BESS) is really heating up, Arun. There's a lot happening in this space, especially with new technologies and the government pushing for more domestic battery manufacturing. But I feel like we need some more expert insight to really get into the details.

Arun: Yeah, BESS is a huge topic, and with everything happening around battery storage and grid stability, it's evolving fast. Who do you think could help us dig deeper into it?

Ankit: [Thinking for a moment] I'm thinking about Rohit Gupta. He's the Business Development Manager at one of the leading lithium battery firms and really knows the battery industry inside out. Plus, he's got a huge network on LinkedIn and keeps up with all the latest trends. I'm sure he could provide some great insights for this chapter.

Arun: That's a great idea. Rohit's well-known in the industry, and he's always sharing updates about market trends and new technologies. He could really help us cover the business side of BESS too.

Ankit: Exactly. He's in the thick of it—he'll know about the investment landscape, where the industry's headed, and what challenges companies are facing right now. I'll reach out to him and see if he's interested in contributing.

Arun: Sounds like a plan. His insights will add a lot of value to this chapter.

Rohit: Hey, Ankit! Great to hear from you. How's everything going?

Ankit: Hey, Rohit! I'm doing well. I'm actually working on my book about India's energy transition, and I've reached the chapter on Battery Energy Storage Systems (BESS). It's a really hot topic, and I thought of you immediately. I was wondering if you'd be open to helping me out with some insights for this chapter.

Rohit: Of course! I'd love to help out. BESS is something I'm deeply involved in, and there's so much happening in that space right now. But before we get into the details, could you walk me through the outline of the chapter? I want to understand what you've covered so far and where I can add value.

Ankit: Sure, let me give you a quick overview. The chapter starts with an introduction to the current status and growth potential of BESS in India, highlighting the installed capacity, government targets, and the market potential up to 2040. Then, I dive into the technological advancements in battery storage —like lithium-ion dominance, emerging technologies like solid-state and flow batteries, and the battery recycling ecosystem.

Rohit: Sounds good so far. What else?

Ankit: Next, I talked about the role of BESS in grid stability and how it addresses the intermittency of renewables, especially in large-scale solar and wind projects. I've included a case study on the Kurnool Ultra Mega Solar Park and its integration with battery storage. Then, there's a section on public and private sector investments in BESS, touching on the PLI scheme, joint ventures, and collaborations with international players.

Rohit: That's a solid structure. But there are a couple of things I think we could expand on. First, in the section about technological advancements, you should mention the cost trajectory of battery storage. Costs have been falling consistently, and I've seen projections that by 2030, we might see prices as low as USD 80 per kWh for lithium-ion batteries. That's a game changer for scaling up BESS.

Ankit: [Writing notes] Good point! I'll add that in.

Rohit: Also, when discussing emerging technologies, it might be worth including something on hybrid storage systems. These combine batteries with other forms of storage, like pumped hydro, to provide both short and long-duration storage solutions. It's becoming a big trend in grid-level applications.

Ankit: Yeah, that's a great idea. Hybrid systems are gaining traction, especially for grid flexibility.

Rohit: One more thing—in the section about investments, you might want to mention the challenges that companies are facing when it comes to scaling up battery production. Supply chain issues for materials like lithium, cobalt, and nickel are still a major hurdle, especially given how dependent India is on imports for these raw materials.

Ankit: You're right. I've touched on the challenges, but I'll expand more on the supply chain constraints and how that affects long-term sustainability for battery manufacturing.

Rohit: Perfect. Overall, the outline looks great. I think with these additional points, it'll cover everything readers need to know about BESS in India—from the current landscape to the future potential. Let me know if you need any more insights as you go along.

Ankit: Thanks so much, Rohit! Your input is exactly what I needed to round out this chapter. I'll make those updates and send you the draft once it's ready.

Rohit: Looking forward to it! Happy to help anytime, Ankit.

As India accelerates its transition toward clean and renewable energy, **Battery Energy Storage Systems (BESS)** have emerged as a cornerstone technology to address the challenges posed by the intermittent **nature of solar and wind power**.

BESS offers a powerful solution by storing excess renewable energy during periods of high generation and releasing it during peak demand or low generation periods. This capability enhances the efficiency and resilience of India's power grid, enabling greater integration of variable renewable energy sources.

This chapter provides an **in-depth exploration of the current status, technological advancements, and future growth potential** of BESS in India. It examines how storage is being deployed to **balance supply and demand, manage peak loads**, and **regulate grid frequency**, while also highlighting the role of **emerging battery technologies** such as solid-state batteries, sodium-ion, and flow batteries in reducing costs and improving performance.

Beyond grid-scale applications, BESS is also revolutionizing **off-grid and rural electrification** by supporting microgrids, electric vehicle (EV) charging stations, and decentralized energy systems. Additionally, the chapter delves into emerging **business models like Energy-as-a-Service (EaaS)** and **peer-to-peer (P2P) energy trading**, which are transforming how storage systems are deployed and monetized.

Key policy initiatives, financial innovations such as **green bonds** and **carbon credits**, and the government's strong push for **domestic battery manufacturing under the Production-Linked Incentive (PLI)** Scheme are further accelerating BESS adoption. However, scaling up storage systems also presents challenges in terms of supply chains, recycling ecosystems, and cost competitiveness.

With India's ambitious target of achieving 500 GW non-fossil fuel capacity by 2030, BESS is poised to become an integral part of the country's **energy security strategy**. This chapter outlines the opportunities, innovations, and obstacles on the path to widespread adoption of battery storage systems, positioning BESS as a **critical enabler of India's energy transition and climate goals**.

Current Status and Growth Potential of BESS in India

India's journey with **Battery Energy Storage Systems (BESS)** has gained significant momentum in recent years, driven by the rapid adoption of renewable energy and the government's strong push for grid modernization.

As of **March 2025, India's operational BESS capacity has reached 4.6 GW/10.5 GWh**, more than doubling in the past two years. This expansion positions India as one of the fastest-growing BESS markets globally.

Image Credit: ANI News

Key Drivers of BESS Adoption

- With renewable energy contributing over 44% of India's installed capacity, BESS is essential for balancing supply and demand, particularly during periods of high solar and wind generation. States like Tamil Nadu, Gujarat, and Rajasthan, which are renewable-rich, are leading in grid-scale BESS deployments to mitigate curtailment issues.

- Grid operators are increasingly deploying BESS for frequency regulation, voltage support, and peak shaving. The Kurnool Ultra Mega Solar Park in Andhra Pradesh now includes a 350 MW/750 MWh battery storage system, one of the largest in Asia.

- Policy support under the National Energy Storage Mission and financial assistance through the Production-Linked Incentive (PLI) Scheme have spurred private investments and encouraged domestic battery manufacturing.

Major Projects and Developments

- Delhi-NCR Grid Balancing Project: A 100 MW/250 MWh grid-scale BESS commissioned in 2024 to provide ancillary services and improve reliability in urban load centers.

- Solar-Wind Hybrid Projects with Storage: Developers like ReNew Power and Adani Green Energy are integrating large-scale BESS into hybrid projects to offer 24/7 renewable power.

- Domestic Manufacturing Surge: India's battery manufacturing capacity has grown to 45 GWh annually, with major facilities in Gujarat and Tamil Nadu.

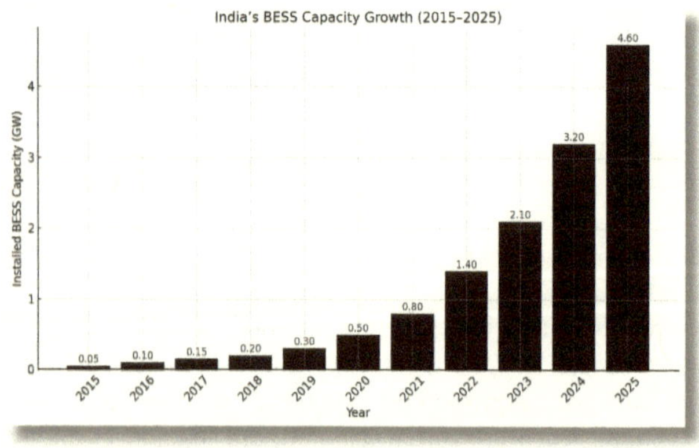

India's BESS market is entering a scaling phase, transitioning from pilot projects to large-scale deployments that are critical for achieving the country's 500 GW renewable energy target by 2030 and ensuring energy security.

Growth Potential:

India's Battery Energy Storage System (BESS) market is entering a rapid growth phase, driven by ambitious renewable energy targets and increasing demand for grid flexibility. The total market potential for BESS in India is now projected to reach USD 9.2 billion by 2027, reflecting strong growth in both utility-scale storage and distributed energy storage systems, such as residential and commercial rooftop solar with battery backup.

By 2040, India's demand for battery storage could surge to 190 GW, fueled by:
- Widespread electrification of transportation, including electric vehicles and charging infrastructure.
- Accelerated deployment of rooftop solar systems with integrated storage.
- The need for grid stability and flexibility to manage high renewable energy penetration, which now accounts for over 44% of India's installed power capacity as of 2025.

Government Policies:

The Indian government has introduced a series of initiatives to accelerate the deployment of Battery Energy Storage Systems (BESS) and strengthen domestic manufacturing capabilities.

The **Production-Linked Incentive (PLI)** Scheme for **Advanced Chemistry Cell (ACC) battery storage**, with an increased outlay of ₹20,400 crore (USD 2.5 billion) in 2024, is a cornerstone of this effort. This scheme aims to create an annual domestic manufacturing capacity of 50 GWh by 2027, reducing India's dependence on battery imports and fostering technological innovation in storage solutions.

Complementing this initiative is the **Green Energy Corridor (GEC)** project, designed to build the transmission infrastructure necessary for integrating large-scale renewable energy projects with energy storage systems. By March 2025, over **20,000 circuit kilometers of transmission lines** have been developed under Phases I and II of GEC, enabling efficient evacuation of renewable energy and supporting grid-scale storage deployment.

Additionally, the **National Energy Storage Mission** (NESM) is working to create a robust ecosystem for energy storage applications in both grid-connected and off-grid systems. This mission supports research and development in next-generation battery technologies, including solid-state, sodium-ion, and flow batteries, which are critical for achieving cost-effective and scalable energy storage solutions in India's clean energy transition.

Technological Developments in Battery Storage Solutions

Technological advancements in battery storage systems are pivotal for making BESS more efficient, cost-effective, and scalable.

The global battery storage market is evolving rapidly, with innovations in battery chemistry, energy density, and recycling.

Lithium-Ion Dominance:

- Lithium-ion batteries (Li-ion) continue to dominate the BESS market due to their high energy density, longer cycle life, and declining costs. As of 2024, the cost of lithium-ion batteries had dropped to USD 110 per kWh, down from USD 135 per kWh in 2021.

- India has been focusing on domestic manufacturing of lithium-ion batteries, with several gigafactories under construction. The Amara Raja and Tata Power plants are expected to significantly increase domestic battery production by 2026.

Emerging Battery Technologies:

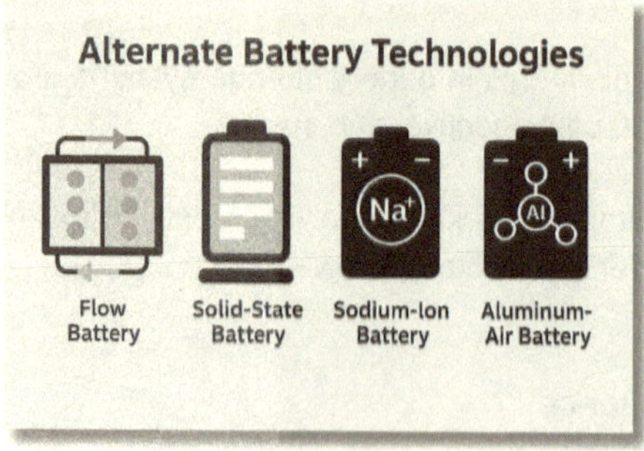

Flow Batteries

Current Market (2025):
- Flow batteries, especially **vanadium redox flow batteries (VRFBs)**, are being deployed in niche **long-duration storage** applications. They are valued for scalability and **extended cycle life (20,000+ cycles)** but face challenges due to high upfront costs and bulky systems. Pilot projects in Gujarat (50 MWh) and Tamil Nadu are underway.

2040 Outlook:
- Flow batteries are expected to capture a **15–20% share of the stationary storage market**, particularly for utility-scale renewable integration and microgrids needing **4–12 hour storage**. Cost reductions from mass production and advancements in electrolyte technology will drive adoption.

Solid-State Batteries

Current Market (2025):
- Still largely in the **R&D and pilot stages**, solid-state batteries promise **2–3x energy density and enhanced safety** compared to Li-ion. Automakers like Toyota and QuantumScape are leading in EV applications, with grid storage commercialization projected within a decade.

2040 Outlook:
- Solid-state batteries could dominate **high-energy applications**, securing 25–30% of global storage markets, including grid-scale and EVs, provided scalability and cost challenges are overcome.

Current Market (2025):
- Sodium-ion batteries are emerging as a **cost-effective alternative** to Li-ion for stationary storage. They offer **lower raw material costs, better thermal stability**, and are ideal for regions where lithium supply is constrained. Pilot deployments are ongoing in Rajasthan and Karnataka.

2040 Outlook:
- Sodium-ion batteries are likely to take a 20–25% share in stationary storage markets, especially in residential, commercial, and rural microgrids. They will complement Li-ion in applications requiring lower energy density but higher safety and affordability.

Current Market (2025):
- Aluminium-air batteries are still in experimental and limited commercial trials. They offer high energy density and are lightweight, but challenges like recharging complexity (need to replace aluminum plates) limit widespread adoption. Startups in India are testing these for EV range extenders.

2040 Outlook:
- If recharging and recycling challenges are addressed, aluminium-air batteries could become a **niche solution for long-duration storage and electric vehicles**, especially in regions seeking metal-based storage solutions. Market share may reach 5–10% in specialized applications.

Grid-Scale Applications: Integrating Renewables with Storage

As India's renewable energy capacity continues to grow—crossing **190 GW** as of March 2025—the need for large-scale energy storage systems has become critical for ensuring grid stability, reliability, and flexibility.

Battery Energy Storage Systems (BESS) are increasingly being deployed alongside solar and wind power plants to manage the variable and intermittent nature of renewable energy.

Balancing Supply and Demand

Grid-scale BESS allows utilities to store excess renewable energy generated during periods of **low demand (e.g., midday solar peaks)** and discharge it during peak demand hours, effectively smoothing out fluctuations in power supply. For example, the **Kurnool Ultra Mega Solar Park in Andhra Pradesh now includes a 350 MW/750 MWh BESS**, which provides load balancing for the regional grid.

Providing Ancillary Services

BESS is playing a crucial role in delivering ancillary services, such as:
- Frequency Regulation: Responding instantly to deviations in grid frequency.
- Voltage Support: Stabilizing voltage levels across the transmission network.
- Black Start Capability: Helping restore grid operations in case of major outages.

Enabling Renewable-Only Round-the-Clock (RTC) Power

Large renewable developers, including **Adani Green Energy** and **ReNew Power**, are now integrating BESS into solar-wind hybrid projects to provide RTC renewable energy to industries and DISCOMs. These projects demonstrate that storage is essential for meeting India's growing demand for **24/7 clean power**.

Scaling Up Storage Capacity

India's operational grid-scale storage capacity has reached 4.6 GW/10.5 GWh as of 2025, with multiple projects under development:

- **Delhi-NCR Grid Balancing Project:** A 100 MW/250 MWh system designed to reduce stress on urban transmission networks.

- **Pavagada Solar Park (Karnataka):** Planning to integrate a 500 MWh storage system to handle excess solar generation.

By 2030, India is targeting 40 GW/120 GWh of grid-scale storage capacity as part of its 500 GW renewable energy goal.

Emerging Business Models: EaaS, P2P Trading, and Distributed Storage

The rapid deployment of Battery Energy Storage Systems (BESS) in India is giving rise to innovative business models that are transforming how energy is produced, stored, and consumed. These models are enabling new revenue streams for developers, enhancing consumer participation in energy markets, and accelerating the transition to decentralized and sustainable power systems.

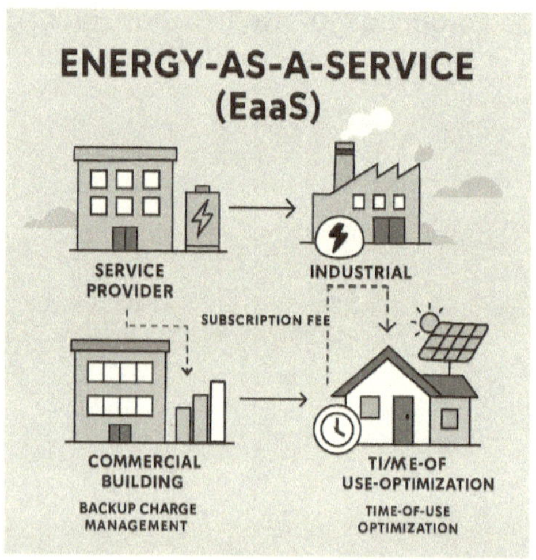

The **Energy-as-a-Service (EaaS)** model allows customers—ranging from industries to residential communities—to access energy storage solutions without large upfront capital investments. In this model, service providers own and operate the battery systems, while customers pay a subscription or usage-based fee.

Applications:
- Backup power for commercial buildings.
- Demand charge management for industrial consumers.
- Time-of-use optimization for residential complexes.

Key Players: Companies like **Tata Power Renewable Microgrid** (TPRM) and **Sungrow** are piloting EaaS offerings in urban and peri-urban areas.

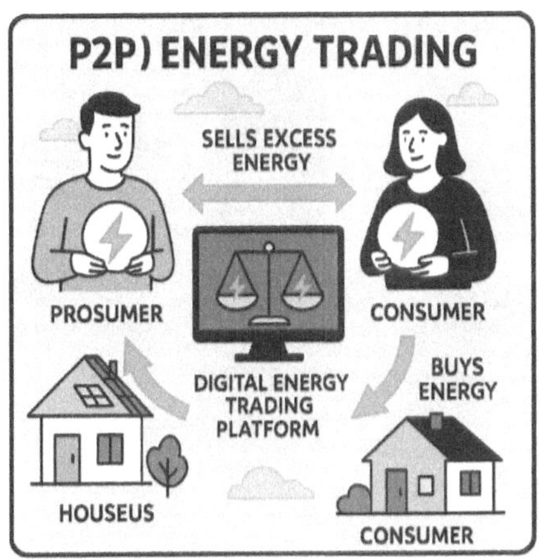

P2P energy trading platforms are emerging as a game-changer for distributed energy systems. With rooftop solar and BESS installations proliferating, consumers (now called "prosumers") can trade surplus energy directly with their neighbors or the local grid using secure digital platforms.

- **Unified Energy Interface (UEI):** The proposed UEI platform in India can enable real-time energy transactions between producers and consumers, enhancing grid efficiency and empowering communities to monetize surplus energy.
- **Pilot Projects:** P2P trading pilots in Delhi and Bengaluru, supported by blockchain technology, are already demonstrating how distributed BESS can participate in local energy markets.

DISTRIBUTED ENERGY STORAGE NETWORKS

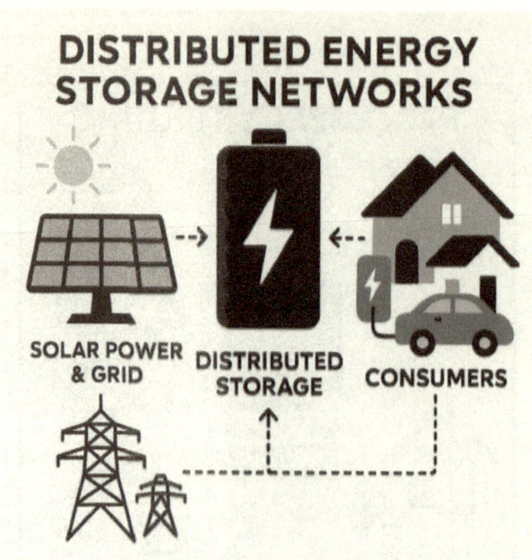

Distributed BESS networks, aggregated through virtual power plants (VPPs), are gaining momentum. These networks coordinate thousands of small-scale batteries to act as a single flexible resource for the grid.

Applications:
- Providing ancillary services to the grid.
- Supporting renewable energy integration.

Future Outlook: By 2030, distributed storage is expected to contribute **10–15% of India's total storage capacity**, driven by smart grid technologies and IoT-enabled systems.

India's embrace of **EaaS, P2P energy trading, and distributed storage networks** marks a paradigm shift from centralized power systems to **decentralized**, consumer-centric energy ecosystems.

These innovations will be critical in unlocking the full value of BESS and supporting the country's journey towards a flexible, low-carbon energy future.

Battery Recycling and Circular Economy Opportunities

As India rapidly scales up its Battery Energy Storage Systems (BESS) and electric vehicle (EV) deployment, managing battery waste has become a critical priority. The push toward a circular economy for batteries is vital for reducing environmental impact, securing critical raw materials, and supporting sustainable growth in the energy storage sector.

Current Status of Battery Recycling in India

India is at the early stages of developing a robust battery recycling ecosystem. By March 2025, the country generates approximately **1.2 lakh tonnes of used batteries annually**, a figure expected to grow exponentially with the proliferation of EVs and grid-scale BESS.

Key players such as **Attero Recycling**, **Gravita India**, and **Lohum Cleantech** are leading efforts to recycle **lithium, cobalt, and nickel** from used batteries. These companies are employing technologies like **hydrometallurgical** and **pyrometallurgical** processes to recover valuable metals and reduce dependence on imports.

Opportunities in a Circular Economy

- Material Recovery and Reuse: Recycling can recover up to 95% of critical materials like lithium, cobalt, and nickel, feeding them back into domestic battery manufacturing.

- Second-Life Applications: Used EV batteries with sufficient residual capacity are being repurposed for stationary storage systems in microgrids and residential backup solutions.

- Policy Support: The Ministry of Environment has implemented the Battery Waste Management Rules (2022), mandating Extended Producer Responsibility (EPR) for battery manufacturers.

By **2030**, India's battery recycling industry is projected to become a **USD 6 billion market**, supporting the country's ambitions for **self-reliant battery supply chains** under the **Atmanirbhar Bharat** initiative. Investments in advanced recycling technologies and local supply chains will be critical for achieving a truly circular energy economy.

Policy Landscape and Financial Innovations Supporting BESS

India's Battery Energy Storage System (BESS) sector is benefitting from a robust policy framework and innovative financing mechanisms aimed at accelerating adoption and reducing costs. Together, these measures are laying the groundwork for a scalable and sustainable energy storage ecosystem.

Policy Landscape

National Energy Storage Mission:
Launched to create a comprehensive framework for energy storage development, NESM focuses on grid integration, R&D support, and domestic manufacturing incentives.

Battery Waste Management Rules (2022):
Mandates Extended Producer Responsibility (EPR), requiring battery manufacturers and importers to ensure collection, recycling, and safe disposal of used batteries.

Production-Linked Incentive (PLI) Scheme for Advanced Chemistry Cell (ACC) Batteries:
With an enhanced outlay of ₹20,400 crore (USD 2.5 billion) in 2024, this scheme supports domestic battery manufacturing and aims to create 50 GWh annual manufacturing capacity by 2027.

Open Access and Time-of-Day Tariffs:
Policies enabling open access to the grid and time-of-day pricing have incentivized industries to deploy BESS for demand charge management and energy arbitrage.

Financial Innovations

Green Bonds:
Indian companies raised over USD 9 billion via green bonds as of March 2025, with a significant share earmarked for grid-scale and distributed storage projects.

Viability Gap Funding (VGF):
The government provides financial support for BESS projects to bridge the gap between capital costs and market viability, particularly for hybrid renewable-storage systems.

Carbon Credits and Energy Trading Platforms:
Innovations like Unified Energy Interface (UEI) and blockchain-based P2P energy trading platforms are enabling BESS owners to monetize surplus energy and earn carbon credits.

Pay-as-You-Go Models:
In rural areas, companies are offering subscription-based BESS solutions that eliminate upfront costs and make storage accessible for microgrids and small businesses.

By combining strong policy backing with innovative financing, India is positioning BESS as a critical enabler of its 500 GW renewable energy target by 2030 and its vision for a net-zero economy by 2070.

India vs Global Leaders in Energy Storage: A Comparative Analysis

As renewable energy takes center stage in global energy strategies, **Battery Energy Storage Systems (BESS)** have emerged as a critical technology for ensuring grid reliability, balancing supply-demand fluctuations, and supporting the electrification of economies. Globally, countries are racing to deploy BESS at scale—not only to integrate variable renewable energy sources like solar and wind but also to pave the way for electric mobility and decentralized energy systems.

India, while still in the **early growth phase**, is positioning itself as a major player in the global BESS market. Understanding how India compares to global leaders offers valuable insights into its opportunities and challenges in this dynamic sector.

China: The Global Energy Storage Giant

China stands as the undisputed leader in battery storage, driven by its aggressive renewable energy expansion and dominance in battery manufacturing.

Installed Capacity (2025): Over 70 **GW/200 GWh**, accounting for nearly 40% of global BESS capacity.

Key Initiatives:
- The "**New Energy Storage Development Implementation Plan (2021–2030)**" targets 100 GW of storage capacity by 2030.
- Mega projects like the **Dalian Flow Battery Energy Storage Station**, a **200 MW/800 MWh vanadium redox flow battery system**, are already operational, showcasing China's focus on long-duration storage technologies.

Strengths:
- Owns over 75% of global battery manufacturing capacity, with giants like CATL and BYD leading innovations in both grid-scale and EV batteries.
- Strong integration of BESS into EV charging infrastructure, enabling smart charging and vehicle-to-grid (V2G) capabilities.

United States: Innovation and Market-Driven Growth

The US is leveraging its technological prowess and market mechanisms to accelerate BESS deployment.

Installed Capacity (2025): Approximately **25 GW/80 GWh**, concentrated in states like California, Texas, and New York.

Key Initiatives:
- California's **Energy Storage Mandate (AB 2514)** requires utilities to deploy 1.3 GW of storage—a goal achieved and surpassed well ahead of schedule.
- The **Moss Landing Energy Storage Facility** in California, one of the world's largest lithium-ion battery systems, now operates at **400 MW/1,600 MWh.**

Strengths:
- Home to pioneering technologies, including solid-state batteries and hydrogen storage systems.
- Robust participation of the private sector, with companies like Tesla Energy and Fluence leading utility-scale deployments.

Future Goals: Double current capacity to **50 GW by 2030** as part of its net-zero roadmap.

European Union: Decentralized and Community-Centric Storage

Europe is building a decentralized energy ecosystem with an emphasis on community-level storage and grid flexibility.

Installed Capacity (2025): Around **18 GW/50 GWh**, led by Germany, Spain, and the UK.

Key Initiatives:
- Germany's **KfW 275 Program** provides subsidies for home solar+battery systems, making residential storage widespread.
- The **Hornsea Project in the UK**, integrating offshore wind with large-scale storage, exemplifies Europe's focus on hybrid systems.

Strengths:
- Focus on distributed BESS and peer-to-peer energy trading platforms.
- Ambitious climate targets under the European Green Deal, aiming for 50 GW of storage by 2030.

India: The Emerging Contender

India's BESS market is still maturing but is growing at an unprecedented pace due to its ambitious renewable energy goals.

Installed Capacity (2025): 4.6 GW/10.5 GWh, with an additional 8 GW under construction.

Key Initiatives:
- The **Green Energy Corridors (Phases I & II)** are laying transmission lines to integrate renewables and storage.
- Large projects like the **Kurnool Ultra Mega Solar Park (350 MW/750 MWh BESS)** and **Pavagada Solar Park BESS (500 MWh)** signal India's intent to scale.

Strengths:
- Government support through the **PLI scheme** and **National Energy Storage Mission (NESM)** is fostering local manufacturing.
- Rapid deployment of off-grid BESS systems for rural electrification.

Future Goals: Reach **40 GW/120 GWh grid-scale storage capacity by 2030**, potentially becoming the third-largest BESS market globally.

Ankit: Hey Arun, this BESS sector really looks promising. It feels like it's on the verge of something big. To me, it's obvious that this sector needs solid backing from both the government and private players to reach its potential. I've been thinking—has anything major happened over the last couple of years that could really shift the game in terms of energy storage or even energy trading?

Arun: Hmm, good question, Ankit. I've been keeping an eye on developments, and I think there's one major policy change that could actually flip the whole game—the delicensing of standalone energy storage systems.

Ankit: Delicensing? I've heard bits about it, but how does it change the landscape?

Rohit: Yes, this is huge! The Ministry of Power's decision to delicense standalone energy storage systems? It's a game changer for BESS. Now, anyone—whether it's a private company, a startup, or even a community initiative—can set up a storage facility without needing to jump through endless regulatory hoops.

Ankit: Okay, so how does that really shake things up? Why is this such a big deal?

Rohit: Here's why—it speeds everything up. Before, if you wanted to build a standalone battery storage system, you had to deal with the bureaucracy, get licenses, wait for approvals—it was a nightmare. Now, with the delicensing, we're going to see a flood of new projects and investments. This will make BESS a lot more attractive to private investors. It doesn't just help with storage, but it could also open up energy trading—allowing stored renewable energy to be sold when the grid needs it most.

Ankit: Wow, so this could make energy trading more viable?

Rohit: Exactly! Think about it. With more storage facilities popping up and no regulatory delays, companies will have the freedom to trade energy, sell it during peak demand, or even export stored energy across borders. This policy basically removes barriers and encourages innovation in the sector.

Battery Energy Storage Systems (BESS) are poised to become the backbone of India's clean energy transition. By mitigating the intermittency of renewable energy, enhancing grid stability, and enabling innovative business models like **Energy-as-a-Service** and **peer-to-peer energy trading**, BESS will redefine how electricity is produced, stored, and consumed across the country.

With robust **public and private sector investments**, rapid **technological breakthroughs** in areas like solid-state and sodium-ion batteries, and a growing ecosystem of supportive government policies, India is charting a path to become one of the global leaders in energy storage.

As India progresses toward its net-zero emissions target by 2070 and aims for 500 GW of renewable energy by 2030, the integration of BESS into the national energy framework is not just a necessity—it is the cornerstone of a resilient, flexible, and sustainable energy future.

If current momentum is maintained, India is well on track to scale up BESS to unprecedented levels and establish itself as a **regional and global hub for energy storage technologies by 2040 and beyond.**

Chapter 7: Energy Efficiency Market of India

- Introduction to Energy Efficiency: A Cornerstone for India's Energy Future

- Government Programs Driving Energy Efficiency

- Role of Energy Service Companies (ESCOs)

- Sectoral Trends and Technologies

- Financing Energy Efficiency

- Consumer-Side Energy Efficiency: Transforming Indian Households and Industries

- Roadmap to 2040: Scaling Energy Efficiency Across Sectors

Energy efficiency has emerged as one of the most powerful yet underappreciated tools in India's quest for energy security and sustainability.

As the country grapples with the challenges of **rapid industrialization, urbanization, and surging population growth,** improving energy efficiency has become the first fuel—a resource that is often cheaper, cleaner, and faster to deploy than building new power plants.

By optimizing the use of existing resources, energy efficiency reduces overall energy demand, lowers emissions, and minimizes reliance on costly fossil fuel imports. In doing so, it enhances India's energy independence while contributing directly to economic growth and environmental sustainability.

This chapter explores how energy efficiency is reshaping India's energy landscape, delving into the **key government programs, market dynamics, and technological advancements** driving this transformation. Flagship initiatives like the **Perform, Achieve, and Trade (PAT)** scheme and the UJALA program have already saved millions of tons of CO_2 emissions and reduced energy consumption across sectors.

The narrative highlights the rise of **Energy Service Companies (ESCOs)**, the growing influence of smart technologies like IoT and AI in energy management, and the critical role of efficiency in **industry, building automation, appliances, and transportation systems**. With innovations such as **BLDC motors, inverter-based technologies, and super-efficient appliances**, India is setting the stage for a massive efficiency revolution.

Finally, this chapter examines the financial innovations and investment mechanisms that are unlocking the full potential of India's energy efficiency market, propelling the nation toward its 500 GW renewable energy target by 2030 and its vision for a net-zero economy by 2070.

Introduction to Energy Efficiency: Importance for Energy Security

Energy efficiency is the practice of delivering the same level of service—whether lighting a home, powering an industrial motor, or cooling a building—using less energy. By eliminating energy waste, it allows countries to meet growing demand without proportionally increasing energy production.

For a country like India, where energy demand continues to grow at an average of 6.5% annually (2025 estimate) due to rapid urbanization and industrialization, energy efficiency is not just an option—it's a necessity. It acts as the **first line of defense** against infrastructure bottlenecks, rising fossil fuel imports, and volatile global energy markets.

Energy Security Impact

By curbing unnecessary energy consumption, India can significantly reduce its reliance on imported oil, coal, and gas, which together account for nearly **35% of India's total energy needs (2025)**. In 2024 alone, energy efficiency interventions helped India **save over 120 million tonnes of oil equivalent (Mtoe)**, directly lowering the import bill and improving the balance of payments.

Furthermore, reducing energy intensity eases pressure on overburdened grids and minimizes the need for large-scale investments in **power generation infrastructure and transmission networks**.

According to the Bureau of Energy Efficiency (BEE), India's energy efficiency programs have already avoided the construction of 33 GW of new generation capacity by March 2025—equivalent to the output of 30 large coal-fired power plants.

Climate Goals

- Energy efficiency is also a linchpin in India's climate commitments under the **Paris Agreement.** The country aims to reduce its **emissions intensity of GDP by 45% by 2030** (compared to 2005 levels), and energy efficiency measures are expected to contribute nearly 40% of this reduction.

- Programs like the **Perform, Achieve, and Trade (PAT)** scheme, the **UJALA LED distribution program**, and the Standards & Labeling initiative have already cut greenhouse gas emissions by 450 million tonnes CO_2 equivalent between 2015 and 2025.

Why Energy Efficiency is India's "First Fuel"?

Unlike adding new power plants or importing LNG, energy efficiency offers an **immediate and cost-effective solution** to meet demand sustainably. Every unit of electricity saved at the consumer's end reduces **2-3 units of energy required at the generation level,** due to transmission and distribution losses.

As India marches toward its goals of 500 GW renewable energy capacity by 2030 and net-zero emissions by 2070, energy efficiency will remain the silent powerhouse driving both economic growth and energy independence.

Government Initiatives: Perform, Achieve, and Trade (PAT) Scheme, UJALA Program

India's journey toward energy efficiency has been propelled by a series of visionary government programs that target energy savings across industries, households, and the public sector.

Two flagship initiatives—the **Perform, Achieve, and Trade (PAT)** scheme and the **Unnat Jyoti by Affordable LEDs for All (UJALA)** program—have not only reduced energy consumption but also generated significant financial and environmental benefits.

Perform, Achieve, and Trade (PAT) Scheme:

Launched in **2012** by the Bureau of Energy Efficiency (BEE), the PAT scheme is a market-based mechanism designed to improve energy efficiency in energy-intensive industries such as iron and steel, cement, aluminum, fertilizers, paper and pulp, and textiles.

- **Coverage & Scale (2025):** The PAT scheme has successfully completed seven cycles, covering 1,250+ large industrial units across 13 energy-intensive sectors.

- Impact:
    - Achieved cumulative energy savings of 22.4 million tonnes of oil equivalent (Mtoe).
    - Avoided 106 million tonnes of CO_2 emissions since inception.
    - Total financial savings estimated at ₹63,500 crore (USD 7.8 billion) for industries.

- **Energy Saving Certificates (ESCerts):** Industries that exceed their energy-saving targets are issued ESCerts, which can be traded with those that underachieve. This has created a vibrant energy efficiency market in India.

- **Global Recognition:** PAT has been lauded as a model program for developing countries by the **International Energy Agency (IEA)**.

UJALA Program (Unnat Jyoti by Affordable LEDs for All)

Launched in **2015**, the UJALA program has transformed India's lighting market and stands as one of the largest energy efficiency initiatives in the world. The program replaced inefficient incandescent bulbs with energy-efficient LED bulbs, fans, and tube lights across households and commercial establishments.

- Scale (2025):
  - Distributed over 420 million LED bulbs, 50 million LED tube lights, and 23 million energy-efficient fans.

- Impact:
  - Annual energy savings of 53 billion kWh, enough to power 4.5 crore Indian homes for a year.
  - Reduction of 44 million tonnes of CO_2 emissions annually.
  - Consumer savings of over ₹24,000 crore (USD 2.9 billion) in electricity bills each year.

- **Expansion:** UJALA has been extended to include smart street lighting programs and solar lantern distribution in rural areas.

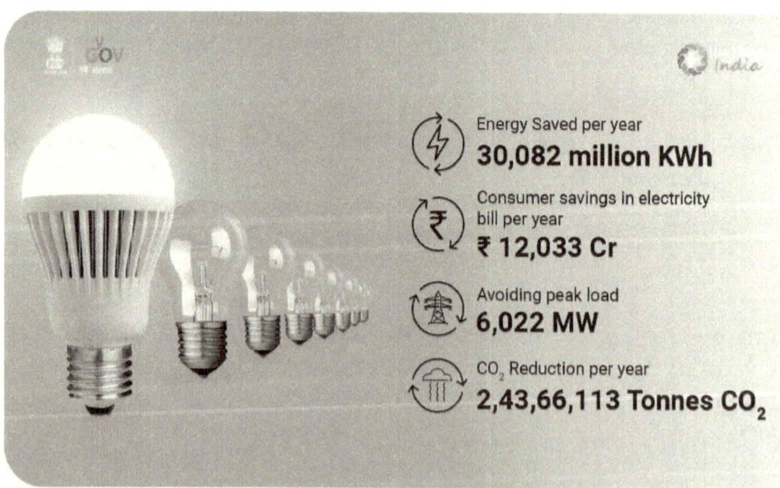

Image Credit: Google

A Global Benchmark

Together, PAT and UJALA have positioned India as a global leader in energy efficiency deployment, demonstrating how large-scale public programs can achieve substantial climate and economic benefits.

As India moves toward its net-zero target by 2070, these programs will remain central to balancing growing energy demand with sustainable practices.

Standards & Labeling Program by Bureau of Energy Efficiency (BEE)

The **Standards & Labeling (S&L) Program**, launched by the **Bureau of Energy Efficiency (BEE)** in **2006**, is one of India's most impactful initiatives to drive energy efficiency in consumer appliances. The program mandates minimum energy performance standards for appliances and provides a star-rating system to guide consumers toward energy-efficient choices.

- Coverage (2025):
    - Over **35 appliances and equipment categories** under mandatory or voluntary labeling, including air conditioners, refrigerators, ceiling fans, water heaters, and televisions.
    - **5-Star labeled appliances** now account for over **70% of total sales** in key categories like air conditioners and refrigerators.

- Impact:
    - Annual energy savings of **75 billion kWh** in 2024-25 alone.
    - Avoided over **62 million tonnes of CO_2** emissions cumulatively.
    - Consumer cost savings estimated at **₹28,000 crore (USD 3.3 billion)** annually.

The S&L program has created a market shift where energy efficiency is no longer a premium feature but a default expectation in Indian households and businesses.

Energy Conservation Building Code (ECBC)

The Energy Conservation Building Code (ECBC), introduced in 2007 and updated in 2017, establishes minimum energy performance standards for new commercial buildings with a connected load of 100 kW or more. The code ensures that buildings are designed to optimize energy use in areas such as lighting, HVAC systems, and building envelopes.

- Coverage (2025):
    - ECBC implementation is now mandatory in 24 states and union territories for commercial buildings.
    - Over 1,200 ECBC-compliant buildings constructed as of March 2025, covering 120 million square meters of built-up area.

- Impact:
    - Buildings adopting ECBC standards are 20–30% more energy-efficient compared to conventional designs.
    - Avoided over 10 million tonnes of CO_2 emissions annually.

The Eco-Niwas Samhita (ENS), a residential version of ECBC, is being implemented for energy-efficient housing developments.

There are 6 types of buildings classified under ECBC:

Hospitality
(i.e. star and no-star rated hotels, resorts)

Educational
(i.e. schools, colleges, universities, training institutions)

Businesses
(i.e. daytime use and 24-hours use- small, medium and large offices based on area)

Assembly
(i.e. theater, transport service facilities, multiplexes)

Healthcare
(i.e. hospitals, out-patient healthcare)

Shopping Complex
(shopping malls, stand-alone retails, open gallery malls, super markets)

Role of Energy Service Companies (ESCOs)

Energy Service Companies (ESCOs) are at the forefront of India's energy efficiency revolution. Acting as enablers, ESCOs provide **market-based solutions** for implementing energy-saving projects across industries, buildings, municipalities, and transportation systems. By identifying efficiency opportunities, executing projects, and recovering investments from the energy savings achieved, ESCOs have created a **self-sustaining ecosystem** for energy conservation.

Emerging Technologies Driving Energy Efficiency

- Smart Meters and Digitalization
    - **Deployment:** Under the **Smart Meter National Program (SMNP)**, India has installed over 28 million smart meters as of March 2025, with a target of **250 million by 2030**.

    - **Impact:** Smart meters allow consumers and utilities to monitor energy use in real time, enable time-of-day tariffs, and reduce transmission and distribution (T&D) losses, which remain around 15% nationally.

- Building Automation Systems (BAS)
    - **Market Growth:** India's green building market is projected to surpass ₹85,000 crore (USD 10.3 billion) by 2025, driven by demand for intelligent lighting, HVAC, and energy management systems in commercial and residential buildings.

    - **Example:** Modern office spaces in cities like Bengaluru and Gurugram use IoT-based BAS to cut energy consumption by up to 35%.

- Waste Heat Recovery (WHR)
    - **Potential:** Indian industries could generate up to 17 GW of electricity from waste heat recovery systems by 2030.

    - **Adoption:** Sectors like cement, steel, and petrochemicals are leading WHR adoption, converting low-grade heat into usable energy and reducing their carbon footprints.

Sectoral Trends and Technologies

Energy efficiency is no longer a one-size-fits-all approach. Each sector—**industry, buildings, transportation**, and appliances—is leveraging tailored technologies and practices to reduce energy intensity and operational costs. These advancements not only enhance productivity but also align with India's broader goals of energy security and sustainability

Industry: The Engine of Energy Efficiency

The industrial sector accounts for nearly 45% of India's total energy consumption (2025). Improving energy efficiency in industries is essential to meeting national climate targets and reducing production costs.

Key Technologies and Trends:

- **Energy-Efficient Motors:** Adoption of BLDC (Brushless DC) motors and IE3/IE4-rated motors in industries like textiles, cement, and chemicals is leading to 20–30% energy savings.

- **Process Optimization:** IoT-based energy monitoring systems are enabling real-time adjustments in manufacturing plants.

- **Waste Heat Recovery (WHR):**
  - Current capacity: 7.8 GW (2025), with potential to grow to 17 GW by 2030.
  - Example: The UltraTech Cement WHR project generates 120 MW from waste heat, offsetting grid power usage.

Buildings: Making Spaces Smarter and Greener

The building sector consumes about 33% of India's electricity, with air conditioning and lighting as major contributors.

Key Technologies and Trends:

- **Building Automation Systems (BAS):** Smart controls for HVAC, lighting, and appliances cut energy use by 25–35%.

- **Green Buildings:** India now has over 10,000 certified green buildings (2025) covering 1.3 billion sq. ft under rating systems like IGBC and GRIHA.

- **High-Efficiency Lighting:** LEDs and motion-sensor systems dominate new commercial projects.

Transportation: Driving Efficiency on Roads and Rails

With growing urbanization, the transportation sector's energy demand is increasing rapidly.

Key Technologies and Trends:
- **Electric Vehicles (EVs):** India crossed 3 million registered EVs in 2025, reducing fossil fuel dependency.

- **Fuel-Efficient Standards:** Mandatory fuel economy standards for cars and commercial vehicles are driving manufacturers toward hybrid and EV technologies.

- **Metro Rail Systems:** Modern metro projects in cities like Delhi, Pune, and Lucknow use regenerative braking systems that recover energy during deceleration.

Appliances and Consumer Electronics: The BLDC Revolution

The appliance sector is undergoing a quiet revolution led by energy-efficient technologies.

Key Technologies and Trends:

- **BLDC Fans:** Now represent 35% of fan sales in 2025, consuming 50% less energy than conventional induction fans.

- **Inverter-Based Appliances:** Widespread adoption in air conditioners, refrigerators, and washing machines due to 5-star energy ratings.

- **Smart Home Ecosystems:** IoT-enabled devices allow consumers to monitor and control energy use remotely.

These innovations, combined with supportive policies like the **Standards & Labeling Program** and **Energy Conservation Building Code** (ECBC), are accelerating India's transition to a low-energy-intensity economy.

Financial Models and Investments in Energy Efficiency

Financing energy efficiency projects has long been a bottleneck in India's energy transition. Unlike renewable energy plants, which generate revenue by selling electricity, energy efficiency projects save money by reducing consumption—making their financial returns less tangible and harder to monetize.

However, innovative financial models, government incentives, and rising private sector participation are now unlocking investments in this critical space.

Government bodies and Institutions associated with Energy Efficiency Financing in India

Performance Contracting: The ESCO Model

- Energy Performance Contracts (EPCs) have emerged as a flagship model for energy efficiency financing in India. Under this model, Energy Service Companies (ESCOs) invest in efficiency upgrades and recover their costs from the energy savings achieved.

Success Stories:
- Widely used in municipal street lighting, where ESCOs retrofit streetlights with LEDs and are paid from the energy savings.

- Example: Under the Street Lighting National Program (SLNP), EPC-based projects have attracted investments worth ₹6,000 crore (USD 720 million) and saved over 11.5 billion kWh annually.

Pay-As-You-Save (PAYS) Models:
These models are gaining traction in household and commercial retrofits. Consumers pay for energy-efficient upgrades (like smart meters or LED appliances) through small increments on their utility bills over time, eliminating upfront costs.

Government Financing and Tax Incentives

- **Accelerated Depreciation:** Businesses investing in energy-efficient equipment can claim accelerated depreciation of up to 40%, reducing their tax liabilities and improving project viability.
- **Capital Subsidies:** Targeted at industries adopting advanced technologies like waste heat recovery and energy-efficient motors.

Private Investment and Green Bonds

The private sector is stepping up to finance energy efficiency through green financial instruments:

Green Bonds:
- India's green bond market has raised over **USD 8.3 billion** (as of March 2025) to finance renewable energy and energy efficiency projects.
- Leading issuers: **NTPC, Adani Green Energy, ReNew Power, and Tata Power.**

International Investments:
- Institutions like the **World Bank, Asian Development Bank (ADB), KfW (Germany), and JICA (Japan)** have funded energy efficiency initiatives in India.
- Areas of investment: **smart grids, building retrofits**, and **energy-efficient public transport systems** (like Delhi Metro's energy optimization programs).

As energy efficiency projects scale across sectors, **blended finance models** (a mix of public and private capital), **green bonds**, and **digital platforms** for energy savings verification will become crucial for attracting large-scale investments.

By 2030, India's energy efficiency market could unlock investments worth over ₹1.5 lakh crore (USD 18 billion), transforming energy conservation from a cost-saving measure into a mainstream investment opportunity.

Arun: Hey Ankit, something just hit me. We've got this whole chapter on energy efficiency, and it's focused mostly on big systems like industrial motors and government initiatives. But this chapter is missing the consumer side—things like BLDC fans, 5-star ACs, and energy-efficient appliances.

Ankit: Hmm, you're right. I haven't touched on that yet. These appliances are a big part of energy efficiency at the household level.

Arun: Exactly. Just look around. People are already using 5-star rated ACs, refrigerators, and even BLDC fans to save energy. And these products are playing a huge role in cutting down electricity bills, which ties directly into the overall theme of energy efficiency. Shouldn't we add a section on this?

Ankit: That's a great point. I need to highlight how these consumer electronics are making a difference, both in homes and industries. Let me add a section on BLDC fans, 5-star appliances, and their role in reducing energy consumption.

Arun: And don't forget the industrial side too—BLDC motors are being used in industrial exhaust fans, which is crucial for factories looking to improve energy efficiency.

Ankit: Absolutely. Let's also dive into how 5-star ratings help consumers make informed decisions and the government programs that are pushing these energy-efficient products.

Consumer-Side Energy Efficiency: Transforming Indian Households and Industries

India's journey toward energy security isn't just about generating more power—it's about using every watt wisely. A key part of this effort lies on the consumer side, where smarter appliances, advanced motor technologies, and behavioral changes are driving an efficiency revolution.

At the heart of this transformation is the adoption of BLDC motors, alongside 5-star rated appliances, which are dramatically reducing electricity demand across households, industries, and even electric vehicles.

The Role of BLDC Fans in Energy Efficiency

BLDC fans (Brushless DC fans) are leading a quiet revolution in Indian homes and offices, proving that small changes can have a big impact.

Efficiency in Homes:
- Traditional ceiling fans with induction motors typically consume 70–80 watts of power. In contrast, BLDC fans consume only 30–35 watts for the same airflow.

- For a household running fans 10 hours a day, switching to BLDC fans can save up to 1,200 kWh annually, cutting electricity bills by ₹1,500–₹2,000 per fan per year.

- In aggregate, if even 25% of Indian households adopted BLDC fans, national savings could exceed 10 billion kWh annually—enough to power a mid-sized city.

Durability and Smart Features:
Modern BLDC fans also come with features like remote controls, timer functions, and even IoT integration, enabling smarter energy use in both homes and commercial spaces.

The Role of BLDC Fans in Energy Efficiency

BLDC fans (Brushless DC fans) are leading a quiet revolution in Indian homes and offices, proving that small changes can have a big impact.

Efficiency in Homes:
- Traditional ceiling fans with induction motors typically consume 70–80 watts of power. In contrast, **BLDC fans consume only 30–35 watts** for the same airflow.

- For a household **running fans 10 hours a day**, switching to BLDC fans can **save up to 1,200 kWh annually**, cutting electricity bills by ₹1,500–₹2,000 per fan per year.

- In aggregate, if even 25% of Indian households adopted BLDC fans, national savings could exceed 10 billion kWh annually—enough to power a mid-sized city.

Durability and Smart Features:
Modern BLDC fans also come with features like remote controls, timer functions, and even IoT integration, enabling smarter energy use in both homes and commercial spaces.

Image Credit: Faradyi

BLDC Motors in Industrial Applications

Industries are also seeing the benefits of switching to BLDC technology in their processes.

Industrial Impact:
- Sectors like manufacturing, HVAC, automotive, and food processing rely heavily on fans, blowers, and pumps. Here, BLDC motors are delivering 30–50% energy savings, translating into substantial cost reductions.

- Example: A textile factory in Coimbatore replaced its traditional HVAC fans with BLDC motors and cut its annual energy use by 40%, qualifying for additional benefits under the PAT (Perform, Achieve, and Trade) Scheme.

Compliance & Rewards:
Industries that adopt BLDC motor-driven systems find it easier to meet PAT targets, earning Energy Saving Certificates (ESCerts) and improving their sustainability scores.

Image Credit: Faradyi

The Importance of 5-Star Rated Appliances

The **Bureau of Energy Efficiency (BEE)'s Star Labeling Program** has made it easier for Indian consumers to identify the most energy-efficient appliances. 5-star rated appliances are now standard in many urban households, helping to reduce India's overall energy intensity.

5-Star Air Conditioners:

- A **5-star AC consumes 20–25% less energy** than a 3-star model.

- Most modern 5-star ACs include inverter technology, adjusting cooling capacity dynamically and avoiding energy wastage during low demand.

5-Star Refrigerators:

- Since refrigerators run **24/7**, energy efficiency is critical. A **5-star refrigerator uses 30–40% less electricity** than a non-rated one, reducing annual energy bills by ₹1,200–₹1,800 per unit.

Other Appliances:

Washing machines, water heaters, and even kitchen appliances are now available in high-efficiency versions, further lowering household energy footprints.

Together, BLDC motors and 5-star appliances are empowering Indian households and industries to cut energy waste, reduce electricity bills, and contribute to national climate goals. As India electrifies further—with more EVs, air conditioners, and appliances entering homes—consumer-side energy efficiency will be the key to keeping demand in check without overburdening the grid.

Roadmap to 2040: Scaling Energy Efficiency Across Sectors

As we look at how far India has come in its energy efficiency journey, it's clear that the last decade has been about laying the foundation—introducing policies, raising awareness, and bringing in affordable technologies like LEDs and BLDC fans.

But looking ahead to **2040**, the challenge and opportunity lie in scaling these efforts across every sector, making efficiency the norm rather than the exception.

This roadmap isn't just about saving energy; it's about redefining how India powers its growth, ensuring we meet rising demand without sacrificing sustainability or energy security.

Consumer and Industrial Engagement: A Cultural Shift

Scaling energy efficiency will require behavioral change alongside technology.

- Consumers: Awareness campaigns, gamification of energy savings (via apps and rewards), and user-friendly energy dashboards will empower individuals to actively manage their energy use.

- Industries: Training programs and knowledge-sharing platforms will help small and medium enterprises (SMEs) adopt best practices in energy management.

Technological Innovation: AI, IoT, and Predictive Efficiency

The next big leap will come from digitalization—embedding intelligence into every device, system, and grid node.

- AI and IoT for Energy Monitoring: Smart sensors and AI-powered analytics will allow households, factories, and utilities to monitor energy use in real time, predict demand spikes, and optimize operations for maximum efficiency.
  - **Example:** AI-driven systems in factories can predict equipment failures and schedule maintenance, reducing downtime and energy waste.

- Predictive Maintenance: IoT-enabled machines will self-diagnose inefficiencies, helping industries avoid energy losses due to worn-out parts or suboptimal operation.

- Smart Homes and Grids: By 2040, most urban households could operate as mini smart grids, capable of dynamically adjusting consumption based on tariff rates and grid conditions.

Vision 2040: Energy Efficiency as India's Second Nature

By 2040, India has the potential to:
- Achieve a **50% reduction in energy intensity of GDP** (compared to 2005 levels).

- Avoid building over 200 GW of additional generation capacity through efficiency alone.

- Save consumers and businesses over ₹5 lakh crore (USD 60 billion) annually in energy costs.

But these numbers, as staggering as they are, will only be realized if India embraces a deeper cultural shift:

If renewable energy is the engine of India's energy transition, then energy efficiency is the steering wheel. Without efficiency, every unit of solar or wind power added to the grid risks being wasted.

To truly secure its energy future, India must recognize that "the cleanest and cheapest unit of energy is the one we never use."

- **Consumers** need to move beyond passive consumption and learn how their choices—from the fans and appliances they buy to how they use them—impact the nation's energy security.

- **Policymakers** must craft stronger, smarter frameworks that make efficiency not optional, but an embedded part of India's growth story.

- **Education systems** should instill energy consciousness from school level, ensuring that tomorrow's citizens are as comfortable talking about kilowatt-hours as they are about kilometers.

Energy efficiency is no longer just an engineering solution; it is a national imperative and a cultural necessity.

If India can achieve this mindset shift, then energy efficiency will become the silent hero in India's quest for energy security—saving more power than any power plant could ever produce.

Energy efficiency is not just a supporting pillar of India's energy security—it is the cornerstone. It offers the most immediate and cost-effective path to reduce energy demand, cut emissions, and ensure the nation's long-term energy independence.

With a robust foundation of government initiatives, expanding market opportunities, and rapid advancements in technologies like BLDC motors, smart meters, and AI-driven energy management systems, India's energy efficiency market is primed for unprecedented growth.

But the real transformation will come when energy efficiency moves beyond being a technical term and becomes a way of life. For this to happen:

- Consumers must be educated about their energy footprints and empowered to make smarter choices.
- Policy frameworks need to evolve into dynamic systems that incentivize efficiency at every level.
- Schools and universities must integrate energy literacy into curricula, nurturing a generation that sees energy not as an unlimited resource, but as a shared responsibility.

If India succeeds in embedding energy efficiency across its homes, industries, and institutions, it will achieve what no amount of imported fuel or new power plants ever could: true energy security and sustainability for over a billion people.

In the quest for a brighter energy future, every saved watt counts—and energy efficiency will be the silent hero driving India forward.

Chapter 8: Challenges in the Indian Power Sector

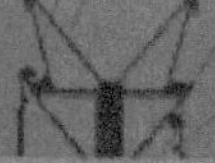

- Transmission and Distribution (T&D) Losses: Causes and Solutions

- Non-Performing Assets (NPAs) in the Power Sector

- Energy Storage Integration Challenges

- Power Theft and its Impact on Energy Security

- Financial Health of DISCOMS: Issues and Reforms

- Energy Banking: A Potential Solution Amidst Challenges

- DISCOM Challenges: Privatization or Govt. Operated

- Policy and Regulatory Bottlenecks in Power Sector Growth

India's power sector continues to stand as the **backbone of the country's industrial and economic growth**, forming a critical pillar in its quest for energy security and sustainable development.

Over the past two decades, the nation has made remarkable progress expanding its installed electricity generation capacity to over **440 GW (as of March 31, 2025)** and achieving near-universal electrification. Yet, despite these achievements, **deep-rooted structural challenges** persist, threatening the efficiency, financial viability, and resilience of the sector.

High transmission and distribution (T&D) losses, the chronic **financial distress of power distribution companies (DISCOMs)**, the growing weight of non-performing assets (NPAs) in the power sector, and power theft remain significant hurdles. Together, they slow India's progress toward building a reliable, modern, and secure energy ecosystem.

As India accelerates its journey toward **grid modernization and electrification**, these challenges are further compounded by **regulatory bottlenecks** and the complex dynamics of integrating renewable energy sources into an already strained grid.

The country's **soaring electricity demand**, coupled with the push for financial sustainability and clean energy adoption, has created a multifaceted set of issues that demand urgent attention.

This chapter explores the **major challenges confronting India's power sector**, incorporating the latest data and developments up to March 31, 2025. It examines the root causes of inefficiencies such as persistently high T&D losses and mounting NPAs while analyzing the reforms underway, including **smart metering rollouts, grid upgrades, DISCOM restructuring**, and emerging **energy storage solutions.**

By addressing these systemic issues head-on, India can lay the groundwork for a resilient, efficient, and financially sustainable power system, capable of supporting its ambitious energy transition and energy security goals for 2030 and beyond.

Ankit: [Holding the draft of Chapter 8] Arun, I'm thinking we should add a new section on the history of Indian energy laws—like a timeline of key regulations and policies that have shaped the power sector since before independence.

Arun: Hmm, but why now? I mean, this chapter already covers a lot about the challenges we're facing today. Why the need for history?

Ankit: I think it's important that readers don't just see the power sector as it is today struggling with T&D losses, financial stress in DISCOMs, or regulatory bottlenecks. They need to understand the journey—the steps we've taken, the roads we've built, and the missteps we've made along the way.

Arun: So, you want to give them a sense of how we got here? The evolution of the sector, not just the problems.

Ankit: Exactly. It's easy to look at the numbers 17% transmission losses, ₹1.9 trillion in NPAs and feel like things are broken. But there was a time when India was struggling even to set up reliable power supply systems, especially before independence. The 1910 Indian Electricity Act laid the first foundation for electricity distribution. Then came the Electricity Supply Act of 1948, which transformed the sector after independence, setting up the State Electricity Boards and creating the backbone for industrial growth.

Arun: You're saying that by looking at the laws, readers will get a sense of how far we've come?

Ankit: Yes! These laws weren't just technical changes. They were turning points in India's industrialization, in our society's shift from agrarian to industrial, and now toward sustainability. Every step, from the 2003 Electricity Act to today's Renewable Energy policies, shows how the sector has adapted to the needs of the nation. We're in a phase where renewables are taking center stage, but that didn't happen overnight.

Arun: I see where you're going with this. It's not just about transmission lines and distribution challenges. It's about how these policies have tried to respond to our growing needs. So, by adding this, readers will understand the philosophy behind energy security.

Evolution of Indian Energy Laws

The regulatory framework governing India's electricity sector has evolved significantly over the past century, transitioning from colonial-era legislation to modern, market-driven reforms aimed at achieving universal access and sustainability.

Indian Electricity Act, 1910

The **Indian Electricity Act of 1910** was the first legislation to provide a regulatory framework for electricity in India. It focused on the **generation, transmission, and distribution of electricity**, laying the foundation for organized electricity supply systems. However, its reach was largely limited to urban areas and private licensees, leaving vast rural regions underserved.

Electricity Supply Act, 1948

After independence, the **Electricity Supply Act of 1948** marked a significant step in reimagining the power sector. It facilitated the creation of **State Electricity Boards (SEBs)** in every state to manage generation and distribution, enabling widespread rural electrification and the development of state-level grids. However, over time, SEBs became plagued by inefficiencies and mounting financial losses, highlighting the need for deeper reforms.

Electricity Act, 2003

The **Electricity Act of 2003** was a watershed moment for India's power sector.

It aimed to:
- Introduce **competition** in generation and distribution.
- Promote **private sector participation**.
- Enable **open access**, allowing large consumers to purchase electricity directly from producers.
- Establish the **Central Electricity Regulatory Commission** (CERC) and **State Electricity Regulatory Commissions** (SERCs) to oversee tariffs and disputes.

This Act paved the way for the unbundling of SEBs and encouraged investments in generation capacity, including renewable energy projects.

National Electricity Policy, 2005

Building on the 2003 Act, the National Electricity Policy (2005) laid out a roadmap to achieve "Power for All" by 2012. It also promoted the integration of renewable energy into the national grid and emphasized reducing transmission and distribution (T&D) losses.

Tariff Policy, 2006

The Tariff Policy established principles for determining cost-reflective tariffs, with the aim of improving the financial health of DISCOMs and incentivizing efficiency in power supply.

National Renewable Energy Policy, 2009

This policy marked India's early commitment to renewable energy, setting ambitious targets to increase the share of solar, wind, and biomass in the national energy mix.

National Energy Policy, 2018

The National Energy Policy (NEP) broadened the focus beyond electricity, aiming for:

- Energy security across all fuel types.
- Universal energy access.
- Promotion of sustainable energy solutions, including electric vehicles (EVs) and energy efficiency measures.

Electricity (Amendment) Bill, 2021 & 2023 Developments

The Electricity (Amendment) Bill, 2021 introduced provisions to:

- Promote renewable energy adoption through Renewable Energy Obligations (REOs) for DISCOMs.
- Improve financial sustainability of DISCOMs via Direct Benefit Transfer (DBT) of subsidies to consumers.
- Enable more competitive electricity markets by allowing multiple supply licensees in a single area.

2023-2025 Updates:
The draft amendments proposed in 2023 further strengthen the framework by introducing:
- National Renewable Energy Grid Code for smoother integration of intermittent renewables.
- Energy Banking and Time-of-Day Tariffs for better demand-side management.
- Provisions for cross-border electricity trade, enhancing regional energy security.

Draft National Energy Policy, 2025 (Ongoing)
The Draft NEP (2025) focuses on:
- Achieving India's net-zero target by 2070.
- Scaling up energy storage solutions (BESS, pumped hydro).
- Creating a National Unified Energy Interface (UEI) to enable seamless energy trading across states and sectors.

Transmission and Distribution (T&D) Losses: Causes and Solutions

India's power sector has made impressive strides in generation capacity and electrification, yet Transmission and Distribution (T&D) losses remain a major Achilles' heel. These losses continue to undermine the sector's efficiency and financial viability, preventing the nation from fully realizing the benefits of its renewable energy push.

As of March 31, 2025, India's national average T&D losses stand at 16.5%, a modest improvement from 17% in 2024, but still significantly higher than the global best practices of 6–8%. This gap highlights the urgent need for reforms and technological interventions to make India's grid leaner and more resilient.

Causes of High T&D Losses:

Technical Losses:

These are inherent in the process of transmitting electricity due to resistance in conductors, transformers, and equipment. However, India's outdated and overstretched infrastructure amplifies these losses:

- Long transmission lines in rural areas, especially in states like Uttar Pradesh and Jharkhand, result in significant voltage drops.
- Poor-quality transformers and overloaded feeders further degrade efficiency.

Non-Technical Losses:

These stem from human and systemic inefficiencies, including:

- Power theft through illegal connections or meter tampering.
- Unmetered agricultural connections, particularly in states like Punjab and Haryana, where free power for farmers often leads to wastage.
- Inaccurate billing and collection inefficiencies, which are rampant in states such as Maharashtra, Rajasthan, and Bihar.

According to recent estimates, **non-technical losses account for 35–40% of total T&D losses** in high-loss regions.

Solutions to Reduce T&D Losses:

Upgrading Infrastructure:
Modernizing the grid is the cornerstone of loss reduction. The **Revamped Distribution Sector Scheme (RDSS)**, launched in 2021, aims to:
- Upgrade aging substations and feeders.
- Build new high-voltage transmission corridors to reduce overloading.
- Target a reduction of T&D losses to **12–13%** by 2027.

Smart Meter Rollout:
Smart meters are transforming electricity distribution by providing:
- **Accurate billing** and detection of energy theft.
- Real-time monitoring of consumption patterns.
- Empowering consumers to manage their energy use better.

As of **March 2025**, India has deployed **40 million smart meters**, with a target of 250 million by 2027. States like **Gujarat** and **Karnataka** have already seen a **10–12% drop in distribution losses** post-deployment.

Underground Cabling in Urban Areas:
Transitioning to underground power cables reduces technical losses and improves system reliability by minimizing faults caused by weather and human interference.
- **Delhi**, **Mumbai**, and **Bengaluru** are pioneering this transition, with Delhi Power Limited (DPL) reporting a **7% improvement in network efficiency** in areas where underground cabling has been implemented.

Artificial Intelligence (AI) for Loss Detection:
Emerging AI-based tools are being piloted in Maharashtra and Tamil Nadu to detect anomalous consumption patterns, helping utilities pinpoint theft and leakages in real time.

Non-Performing Assets (NPAs) in the Power Sector

The issue of **non-performing assets (NPAs)** has long plagued India's power sector, particularly in the **thermal generation segment**, threatening the financial stability of both lenders and producers. While the country has made remarkable strides in expanding its power capacity, this growth has come at a cost: an alarming rise in stressed assets.

As of **March 31, 2025**, the total NPAs in India's power sector stand at approximately **₹1.8 trillion (USD 21.6 billion)**, marginally lower than the **₹1.9 trillion recorded in 2024**. This figure still accounts for 8.5% of the banking system's total NPAs, reflecting how deeply the power sector's financial health is intertwined with the broader economy.

Causes of NPAs in the Power Sector:

Overcapacity in Thermal Power:
- During the early 2000s, India pursued an **aggressive thermal power expansion strategy**, driven by ambitious demand projections. However, actual electricity demand growth has lagged, leaving several plants under-utilized.
- The **average Plant Load Factor** (PLF) of thermal plants dipped further to **54% in 2024-25**, compared to **56% in 2023-24**, worsening the financial stress on generation companies (GENCOs).

Fuel Supply Challenges:
- Many coal-based projects suffer from inconsistent domestic coal supply and delays in securing long-term fuel linkages.
- Gas-based plants, particularly in southern and western India, remain stranded due to declining domestic gas production and high international LNG prices.

Debt-Heavy Financing Models:
- Power projects, especially those led by private developers, were financed with high debt-equity ratios.
- Cost overruns, land acquisition delays, and slower returns on investment have led many such projects into default.

Asset Restructuring and Resolution:
- Banks and financial institutions, in collaboration with developers, are restructuring stressed assets to restore viability.
- The **National Asset Reconstruction Company (NARCL)**, operational since 2022, has taken over ₹**45,000 crore (USD 5.4 billion)** worth of stressed power projects as of March 2025 for resolution.

Shift Towards Renewable Energy:
- Renewable energy projects have emerged as a safer bet for investors:
  - Minimal fuel supply risks.
  - Faster commissioning timelines.
  - Predictable cash flows due to **power purchase agreements (PPAs)**.
- As a result, there's a gradual shift in capital flows from thermal to solar, wind, and hybrid energy projects, reducing the overall NPA burden in the sector.

Policy Interventions:
- The government's **Late Payment Surcharge Rules (2022)** and efforts to improve the financial health of DISCOMs have reduced payment delays, indirectly alleviating pressure on generation companies.
- The **Draft Electricity (Amendment) Bill, 2025** proposes mechanisms to ensure timely payments from buyers to power producers, which could further mitigate stress.

Energy Storage Integration Challenges

As India rapidly expands its renewable energy capacity, with over **190 GW of solar and wind power installed as of March 31, 2025**, a new set of challenges has emerged—integrating these intermittent sources into the national grid. Solar and wind power are inherently variable, dependent on weather and time of day, which creates peaks and troughs in generation that traditional grids were never designed to handle.

Grid Stability Concerns

Renewable energy sources, unlike coal or gas-based plants, **cannot guarantee consistent supply** around the clock. For example:
- **Solar power** peaks during the daytime but drops to zero at night.
- **Wind power** is subject to seasonal and geographic variations.

This intermittency often leads to situations where **surplus generation during peak hours** cannot be absorbed by the grid, while **deficits during low generation periods** create stress on baseload power plants. Without robust balancing mechanisms, these fluctuations risk causing frequency deviations, voltage instability, and even blackouts in extreme cases.

States like **Tamil Nadu** and **Gujarat**, which lead in renewable energy deployment, frequently face grid congestion issues, especially during high wind generation periods.

Energy Storage: The Missing Link

The integration of **large-scale energy storage systems** is critical to overcoming these challenges. While progress has been made in deploying **Battery Energy Storage Systems** (BESS) and exploring pumped hydro storage, India's current capacity falls short of the scale required.

- **Battery Energy Storage Systems (BESS):** As of March 2025, India has installed 5 GW/12 GWh of BESS capacity, primarily in renewable energy-rich states like Maharashtra, Karnataka, and Rajasthan.
    - **Example:** The Khavda BESS project in Gujarat (500 MW/1 GWh) is helping manage surplus solar generation from the Khavda Solar Park.

- **Pumped Hydro Storage:** India's operational pumped hydro capacity stands at **4.9 GW**. New projects like the Tehri PSP (1 GW) are under construction but face environmental and land acquisition hurdles.

Power Theft and its Impact on Energy Security

Power theft remains one of the **most persistent challenges** in India's power sector, directly contributing to high Transmission and Distribution (T&D) losses and undermining the financial viability of distribution companies (DISCOMs).

Despite decades of reforms and electrification efforts, illegal connections, meter tampering, and energy pilferage continue to plague both urban and rural areas, creating a vicious cycle of losses and poor service delivery.

Scale of Power Theft:

As of **March 2025**, power theft accounts for approximately **18–22%** of non-technical losses, resulting in **annual revenue losses of ₹19,500 crore** (USD 2.34 billion) for DISCOMs nationwide.

- States with the highest incidence of power theft include:
    - Uttar Pradesh: Some districts report theft levels exceeding 40% of total distributed electricity.
    - Maharashtra: Urban slums and rural agricultural areas see widespread meter tampering and unauthorized tapping.
    - Bihar and Rajasthan: High rates of unmetered connections and bypassed meters exacerbate losses.

The impact of such theft extends far beyond lost revenue, threatening the overall energy security of the country.

Impact on Energy Security

Financial Stress on DISCOMs:
Power theft directly erodes DISCOM revenues, preventing them from recovering the full cost of power generation and supply. As of 2025, cumulative DISCOM debt has risen to ₹6.4 trillion (USD 77 billion), and theft remains a major contributing factor. This financial distress hampers their ability to:
- Upgrade infrastructure.
- Invest in modern technology like smart grids.
- Pay power producers on time, creating a domino effect across the sector.

Load Shedding and Poor Service Quality:
High theft levels force DISCOMs to **ration electricity** in theft-prone areas to limit losses, leading to **frequent load shedding** and unreliable power supply. This, in turn, affects industries, hospitals, and households, perpetuating dissatisfaction among consumers.

Barriers to Renewable Energy Integration:
 Power theft complicates the integration of renewable energy into the grid, as fluctuating demand and revenue leakages make grid balancing more difficult.

Measures to Combat Power Theft

Smart Metering:
Smart meters are at the forefront of anti-theft strategies, enabling:
- Real-time consumption monitoring.
- Detection of meter tampering and unauthorized connections.
- Prepaid billing options to eliminate unpaid dues.

As of March 2025, India has deployed 40 million smart meters, with theft-prone states like Haryana and Madhya Pradesh reporting 10–15% reductions in non-technical losses in pilot areas.

Strict Penalties and Legal Reforms:
Several states have strengthened laws to penalize offenders:
- Uttar Pradesh Power Corporation Limited (UPPCL) has implemented fines up to ₹1 lakh and imprisonment for repeat offenders.
- Haryana runs "Bijli Chori Nivaran" campaigns, combining legal action with awareness drives to encourage legal connections.

AI-Powered Detection Systems:
In 2024–25, **AI-based theft detection algorithms** were piloted in **Maharashtra** and **Delhi**, helping utilities identify suspicious consumption patterns and proactively address leakages.

Community Engagement:
Programs encouraging local communities to report theft anonymously, coupled with subsidized legal connections for low-income households, have seen success in parts of West Bengal and Kerala.

Financial Health of DISCOMS: Issues and Reforms

The financial fragility of India's power distribution companies (DISCOMs) continues to pose one of the most significant threats to the country's energy security and the viability of its power sector.

Despite repeated bailout packages and structural reforms, DISCOMs remain trapped in a cycle of high debt, operational inefficiencies, and revenue shortfalls, undermining their ability to invest in modernization and reliably serve consumers.

As of March 31, 2025, the cumulative debt of India's DISCOMs has climbed to **₹6.4 trillion (USD 77 billion)**, reflecting a slight increase from 2024 levels. Unless addressed comprehensively, this financial stress threatens to derail India's clean energy ambitions and grid modernization efforts.

Key Issues Facing DISCOMs:

Revenue Gaps (ACS-ARR Mismatch):
- The **Average Cost of Supply (ACS)** continues to exceed the **Average Revenue Realized (ARR)** across most states.
- As of 2025, the national **ACS-ARR gap** stands at **₹0.48/kWh**, a marginal improvement from ₹0.50/kWh in 2024, but still unsustainable.
- This gap is exacerbated by delays in tariff revisions and high levels of technical and commercial losses.

Subsidized Tariffs and Political Pressures:
- Free or heavily subsidized electricity for agriculture and residential consumers in states like Punjab, Rajasthan, and Maharashtra contributes to massive revenue shortfalls.
- For example, Punjab provides free electricity to farmers, resulting in an annual subsidy burden exceeding ₹15,000 crore (USD 1.8 billion).

High T&D Losses:
Many DISCOMs, especially in Uttar Pradesh, Bihar, and Jharkhand, face combined technical and commercial losses of 25–30%, far above the national target of 15%.

Delayed Payments to Generators:
Cash-strapped DISCOMs often delay payments to power generators, creating liquidity crunches across the power sector.

Reforms to Improve Financial Health

Revamped Distribution Sector Scheme (RDSS):
Launched in 2021, the RDSS is a flagship initiative designed to:
- Improve operational efficiency and financial sustainability.
- Provide ₹3.04 trillion (USD 36.4 billion) in grants and loans for:
  - Infrastructure modernization (feeder segregation, transformer upgrades).
  - Loss reduction initiatives.
  - Smart meter deployment (target: 250 million smart meters by 2027).

Tariff Reforms:
- The government has directed states to:
  - **Gradually reduce electricity subsidies** and replace them with **Direct Benefit Transfers (DBTs)** to ensure financial discipline.
  - Implement cost-reflective tariffs that recover the full cost of supply.
  - Roll out Time-of-Use (ToU) tariffs, incentivizing consumers to shift demand away from peak hours.

Payment Security Mechanism:
- The **Late Payment Surcharge Rules** (LPS) introduced in **2022** require DISCOMs to pay penalties for delayed payments to generators.
- As of 2025, this mechanism has reduced payment delays by 30%, ensuring improved cash flows for generation companies.

Privatization and Franchisee Models:
- States like Odisha and Union Territories have pioneered the privatization of distribution utilities, resulting in better billing efficiency and reduced losses.

Energy Banking: A Potential Solution Amidst Challenges

As India scales up its renewable energy capacity, **energy banking** has emerged as a promising tool to **optimize renewable energy utilization** and stabilize the power grid. By enabling renewable energy producers to "deposit" surplus energy during periods of high generation (like sunny afternoons or windy nights) and "withdraw" it during low generation periods, energy banking offers a pathway to smooth out intermittencies inherent in solar and wind power.

This mechanism not only enhances **grid flexibility** but also supports open access consumers and industries in managing their energy needs efficiently. However, while energy banking holds immense potential, there are several hurdles to overcome for widespread adoption.

Key Challenges in Energy Banking

Regulatory Framework Gaps:
Currently, energy banking policies vary significantly across states, creating **ambiguity for developers and consumers.**

- Some states, like **Karnataka** and **Tamil Nadu**, have introduced monthly or annual energy banking provisions, while others have no defined policies.

- A **national regulatory framework** is urgently needed to standardize practices, define banking periods, and clarify charges to ensure investor confidence.

Infrastructure Limitations:
India's existing grid infrastructure, particularly in rural and remote regions, is often outdated and ill-equipped to manage the complexities of energy storage and redistribution.

- Without smart grids and flexible transmission systems, large-scale energy banking will remain a challenge.

Consumer Awareness:

Energy banking is still a relatively **new concept** for most consumers, industries, and even some utilities.

- Building awareness about its benefits, cost savings, and operational models will be critical to drive participation from all stakeholders.

Financial Viability:

High upfront investments for storage infrastructure (such as Battery Energy Storage Systems (BESS) and pumped hydro storage) and associated grid upgrades have raised concerns about financial feasibility.

- Developing **innovative business models** like **Energy-as-a-Service (EaaS)** and offering incentives or subsidies will be essential to attract private capital.

Inter-State Coordination:

With renewable energy projects often concentrated in a few states, ensuring seamless inter-state energy banking will require policy alignment across state boundaries.

- For example, surplus solar energy from **Rajasthan** must be efficiently banked and transmitted to demand centers in Delhi or Maharashtra.

DISCOM Challenges: Privatization or Govt. Operated

The debate over whether India's power distribution companies (DISCOMs) should remain state-operated or move towards privatization is at the heart of discussions on reforming the power sector.

Both models present unique advantages and challenges, particularly in the context of India's financially stressed and operationally inefficient distribution system.

Financial Health: Strained State DISCOMs vs. Agile Private Players

Government-Operated DISCOMs
State-operated DISCOMs continue to struggle under a mountain of debt and chronic revenue gaps:

- As of **March 31, 2025**, their cumulative debt has risen slightly to **₹6.4 trillion (USD 77 billion)**, reflecting persistent financial stress despite bailout schemes.

- **Heavy subsidies** for agriculture and residential consumers in states like **Punjab, Tamil Nadu**, and **Maharashtra** further strain their finances.

- Political pressures often prevent **cost-reflective tariff hikes**, leaving state DISCOMs unable to recover the full cost of supply.

Privatization: A Path to Financial Discipline?
Private players bring a commercial approach focused on efficiency and cost recovery.

- Success stories like **Delhi's privatization in 2002** demonstrate how private DISCOMs can:
    - Reduce **AT&C losses** (Delhi brought losses down from 55% in 2002 to 7% in 2025).
    - Improve service quality and 24/7 reliability.

- However, privatization remains politically contentious in states where electricity subsidies are seen as a welfare tool.

- Fear of tariff hikes and loss of government control often triggers public protests, as seen in Odisha's privatization efforts in the late 1990s.

Government-Operated DISCOMs
State-run DISCOMs are often hampered by:
- Bureaucratic inertia and delays in decision-making.

- Outdated infrastructure and minimal investment in smart technologies like smart meters, automated billing, and GIS mapping.

- Limited capacity to tackle power theft, which remains high in regions like Uttar Pradesh and Bihar.

Privatization and Modernization
Private DISCOMs are better positioned to:
- Invest in modern infrastructure and smart grids.

- Deploy smart meters, enabling real-time monitoring and significant reductions in theft and technical losses.

- Improve customer service, with online payment systems, app-based outage reporting, and predictive maintenance.

However, large-scale privatization must be handled with careful regulatory oversight to avoid monopolistic practices and ensure service affordability.

Policy and Regulatory Bottlenecks in Power Sector Growth

India's power sector has made impressive strides in **expanding generation capacity**, achieving near universal electrification, and integrating renewable energy into its energy mix. Yet, policy and regulatory hurdles continue to impede its progress, creating friction points that undermine efficiency, investment flow, and innovation.

As India targets 500 GW of renewable energy by 2030, addressing these bottlenecks is crucial to unlock the sector's full potential.

Regulatory Delays

Clearances for Power Projects:
- Environmental approvals, land acquisition, and multiple regulatory clearances remain major hurdles for large-scale projects, particularly thermal and hydro power plants.

- As of March 2025, over 12 GW of planned capacity additions are stalled due to clearance delays, including:
  - The **Etalin Hydropower Project** in Arunachal Pradesh (stuck in environmental litigation).
  - Multiple thermal power plants in Chhattisgarh and Odisha, awaiting forest and land approvals.

Transmission Infrastructure Approvals:
- High-renewable states like Rajasthan and Gujarat struggle with delays in transmission line approvals due to:
  - Land disputes.
  - Protests over rights of way (RoW).
  - Environmental clearances in ecologically sensitive zones.

This bottleneck is particularly damaging as renewable energy projects depend on **evacuating power to demand centers** far from generation sites.

Coordination Between Central and State Governments

The Indian power sector operates under concurrent jurisdiction, where both central and state governments hold authority over critical issues such as:
- Tariffs
- Subsidies
- Project Approvals

This dual control frequently leads to policy inconsistencies and project delays.
- For instance:
  - In Andhra Pradesh, a reversal of signed Power Purchase Agreements (PPAs) for renewable energy projects in 2023 shook investor confidence.
  - Conflicting subsidy policies between central and state governments continue to create hurdles in renewable energy rollouts.

India's power sector stands at a critical crossroads. While remarkable progress has been made in expanding generation capacity, achieving near-universal electrification, and integrating renewable energy into the grid, deep-rooted structural challenges continue to weigh down its full potential.

High transmission and distribution (T&D) losses, the financial distress of DISCOMs, mounting non-performing assets (NPAs) in the generation segment, rampant power theft, and persistent policy and regulatory bottlenecks threaten to undermine the sector's sustainability and its ability to meet the demands of a growing economy.

Addressing these challenges requires a multi-pronged and coordinated effort involving the government, regulators, private investors, and technology innovators.

Key priorities include:
- Restoring financial sustainability of DISCOMs through tariff rationalization, targeted subsidies, and operational reforms.
- Modernizing infrastructure with investments in smart grids, energy storage systems, and advanced metering technologies.
- Simplifying regulatory frameworks and ensuring better coordination between central and state authorities to unlock investment and accelerate project implementation.

As India moves toward its ambitious goal of a net-zero energy system by 2070 and a 500 GW renewable capacity by 2030, a robust and resilient power sector will be the bedrock of this transition.

The next decade presents an opportunity to transform these challenges into catalysts for innovation and reform, ensuring affordable, reliable, and sustainable power for all Indians—the true cornerstone of India's energy security and economic growth.

Ankit (leaning back in his chair): Finally, we're done with this chapter. That was a heavy one lots of moving pieces in the power sector. How do you feel about it?

Arun: Honestly, it's a solid breakdown of all the critical challenges, from T & D losses to NPAs. But what hit me was that energy laws timeline you added. It gives the whole chapter a sense of history and progress. We don't often realize how much the laws and policies shape the current issues passed decades ago.

Ankit: Exactly. That's what I was hoping to capture. When you look at the challenges today, especially the regulatory bottlenecks and financial health of DISCOMs, it all makes more sense when you trace the journey back. The struggle isn't just about modernization, but about how we've evolved as a sector over the past century.

Arun: It's like connecting the dots. We're still dealing with some of the same core issues, like power theft and infrastructure weaknesses, but now we've got modern solutions like smart meters and privatization on the table.

Ankit: Exactly. The fact that we're adding content on energy banking, cross-border trade, and DISCOM privatization makes this chapter even more relevant to today's discussions. This chapter shows that even though the challenges are complex, there are so many growth opportunities.

Arun: Well, after going through all of this, I'm glad we're moving forward. But I think this is one chapter readers will need to sit with for a while—it covers so much ground.

Ankit: True, but that's the point. We want them to see the full picture. Challenges, yes—but also the opportunities, the untapped potential, and the ongoing reforms. Hopefully, it gives them some perspective.

Arun: Absolutely. It feels like we've not only highlighted the problems but also set the stage for the solutions.

Ankit: Alright then, I think this chapter is ready to be wrapped up. Let's move on to the next challenge, shall we?

Arun: Onward and upward.

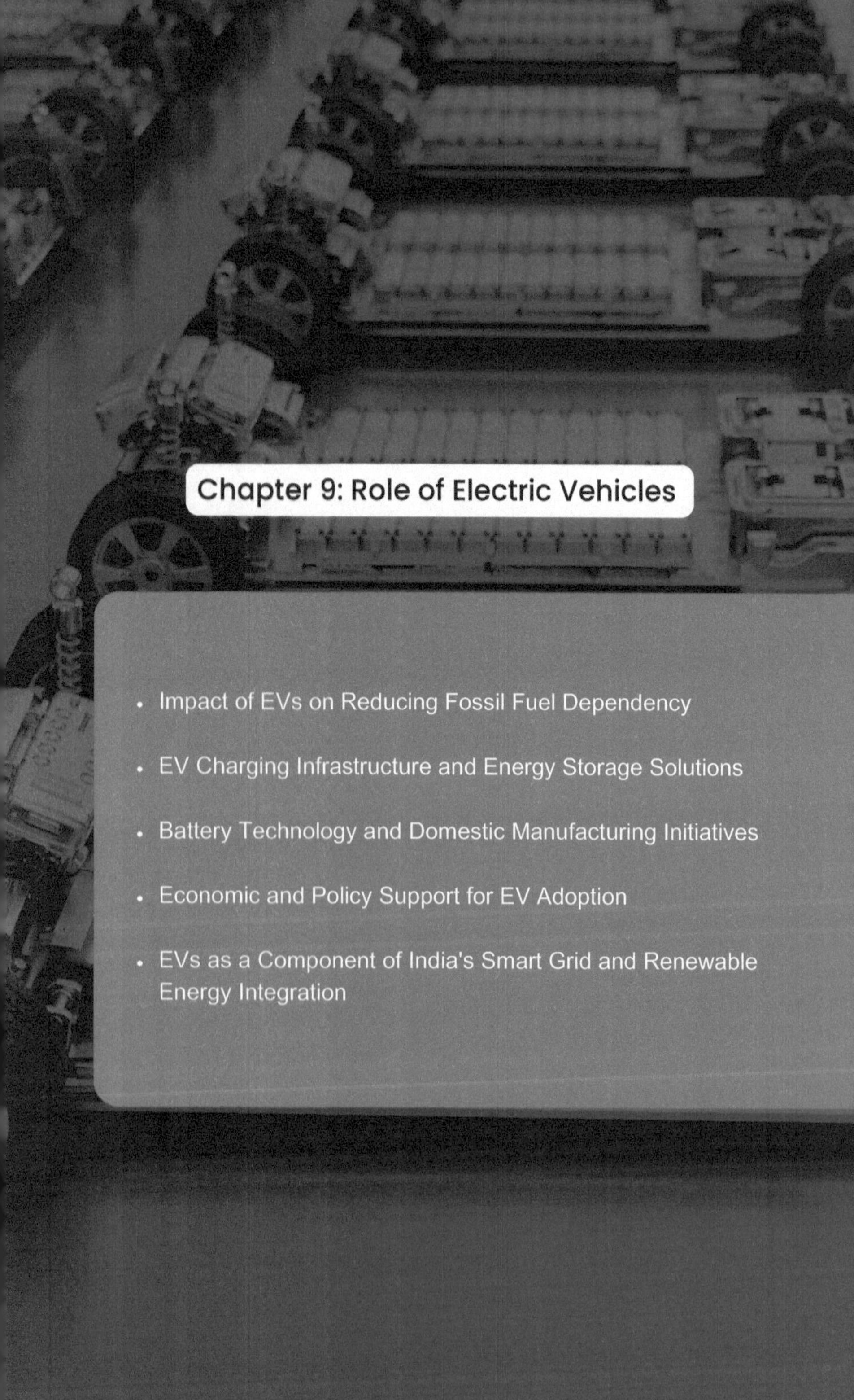

Chapter 9: Role of Electric Vehicles

Impact of EVs on Reducing Fossil Fuel Dependency

EV Charging Infrastructure and Energy Storage Solutions

Battery Technology and Domestic Manufacturing Initiatives

Economic and Policy Support for EV Adoption

EVs as a Component of India's Smart Grid and Renewable Energy Integration

Ankit (sitting at his desk, flipping through some notes): Arun, I think it's time you got directly involved in the content of this book. You've been handling the social media marketing of All India EV for over 2.5 years now. You've got a solid grip on the pulse of the EV industry, and I feel like you could bring in some fresh insights.

Arun: You know I've been dying to jump into this project for a while. It's exciting to see how far the EV industry has come, especially in India, and there's so much happening right now. But, what exactly do you want me to do?

Ankit: This chapter is about the role the EV industry is playing in India's journey toward energy security. I need your input, your perspective from all the work you've done managing the social media and tracking industry updates. The way you've connected with the audience and the industry leaders gives you an edge.

Arun: All right, I see what you're getting at. I've been following all the market trends closely—the rise in EV sales, charging infrastructure updates, and even the battery innovations. There's so much happening, and the government's push is stronger than ever. I'd love to help with this chapter, bringing in some of the nuances and strategies I've seen while running All India EV.

Ankit: Exactly. I want you to go beyond just technical details and help me communicate the excitement and challenges of the EV space, especially for our audience. Let's make this chapter a blend of detailed insights and the larger vision.

Arun: You've got it. Let's break down how the EV industry is transforming our energy security, from cutting down on oil imports to driving renewable energy integration. And we can't forget the charging infrastructure India's really scaling up on that front.

Ankit: Perfect! Let's make this chapter not only informative but inspiring for readers who might be new to this space. The goal is to show them the bigger picture how the EV revolution fits into India's quest for energy security.

Impact of EVs on Reducing Fossil Fuel Dependency

As of March 31, 2025, India's rapidly expanding electric vehicle (EV) market has emerged as a key driver in reducing the nation's dependence on fossil fuels, particularly imported crude oil. India still imports approximately 83% of its crude oil requirements, with nearly 40% of that oil consumed by the transportation sector. The widespread adoption of EVs, powered largely by domestically generated electricity and increasingly by renewable sources, is helping to curb this reliance, improving the country's energy security and saving valuable foreign exchange reserves.

EV Adoption Impact

By early 2025, India had surpassed **3.6 million EVs** on its roads, spanning electric **two-wheelers, three-wheelers, passenger cars**, and **buses**. This transition has already:

- Reduced annual fossil fuel consumption by an estimated **2.9 million barrels of oil equivalent**.
- Saved approximately ₹20,000 crore (USD 2.4 billion) in oil import costs during FY 2024–25.

This growing EV fleet is also enabling India to decarbonize its transport sector, aligning with global climate goals.

Carbon Emission Reduction

The increasing share of EVs has led to an annual reduction of nearly 18 million tonnes of CO_2 emissions as of 2025. This directly supports India's commitments under the Paris Agreement to cut its emissions intensity by 45% by 2030 and achieve net-zero by 2070.

Projected Impact by 2030

At current growth rates and with additional policy support:

- EV adoption could reduce India's crude oil imports by 32–37% by 2030.
- Annual CO_2 emission reductions from EVs alone could exceed 75 million tonnes, a significant contribution to India's clean energy transition.

Government Policies Driving EV Growth

FAME II and FAME III Transition:
- Under the Faster Adoption and Manufacturing of Hybrid and Electric Vehicles (FAME II) scheme, subsidies for EVs and charging infrastructure have been pivotal.

- By March 2025:
    - 1.8 million electric two-wheelers,
    - 850,000 electric three-wheelers,
    - 25,000 electric buses were deployed with FAME II support.

- The draft FAME III policy, expected in 2025, aims to:
    - Extend incentives for EV batteries with advanced chemistries (like sodium-ion and LFP).
    - Focus on tier-2 and tier-3 cities for charging infrastructure expansion.

Draft National Automotive Policy (2025):
The revised draft policy targets:
- 40% EV penetration in private cars.
- 80% in two-wheelers.
- 75% in commercial vehicles by 2030.
- It also includes:
- Production-linked incentives (PLI 2.0) for local battery manufacturing.
- Tax exemptions and GST reductions for EV makers and buyers.

Critical Mining and Supply Chain Security

India's dependence on imported lithium, cobalt, and nickel poses a strategic challenge. In response:

- Bilateral agreements have been signed with **Australia**, **Argentina**, and **Bolivia** for securing lithium supplies.

- The **Geological Survey of India** (GSI) announced the discovery of 5.9 million tonnes of lithium reserves in Jammu & Kashmir in 2023.

- The government plans to launch a Critical Minerals Mission to develop domestic mining and processing capabilities.

These efforts are vital for ensuring energy security and supporting the local battery manufacturing ecosystem.

EV Charging Infrastructure and Energy Storage Solutions

A robust charging infrastructure is the backbone of India's electric mobility revolution. As the number of electric vehicles (EVs) on Indian roads continues to grow, ensuring convenient, fast, and sustainable charging solutions has become a national priority. Parallelly, the integration of energy storage systems (ESS) is emerging as a critical enabler for both grid stability and renewable energy adoption, ensuring that EVs are powered cleanly and efficiently.

Charging Stations: Expanding the Network

By March 31, 2025, India's public charging network had expanded to 92,000 charging stations, up from 75,000 in August 2024—a growth driven by government mandates and private sector investments.

Ultra-Fast Charging Infrastructure
- Over 3,000 ultra-fast charging stations (>150 kW) have been installed along major highway corridors like Delhi-Mumbai Expressway and Bengaluru-Chennai corridor.
- These stations allow EVs to charge up to 80% in 20–30 minutes, addressing range anxiety for inter-city travel.

2030 Target
The government aims to deploy 150,000 public charging stations nationwide by 2030, with a special focus on tier-2 and tier-3 cities to promote equitable EV adoption.

India's EV charging ecosystem is moving rapidly towards global and national standards to ensure widespread adoption and user convenience.

- **Bharat EV Charger Standards** (AC-001, DC-001) cater to low-power applications, mainly for two-wheelers, three-wheelers, and affordable four-wheelers.

- **Combined Charging System (CCS2)** has been adopted as the preferred standard for high-speed DC fast charging in India, in line with global practices.

- Draft guidelines emphasize interoperability and the **development of a Roaming Charging Network**, allowing EV users to charge across different networks seamlessly with a single account or app.

These measures are critical for building consumer confidence, reducing range anxiety, and enabling large-scale EV adoption.

Battery Swapping: Fast, Flexible, and Scalable

Battery swapping has emerged as a game-changer for two-wheelers, three-wheelers, and small commercial EVs, where time and operational efficiency are critical.

As of 2025, over 2,100 battery swapping stations operate in 70+ cities.
Battery swapping reduces the downtime for EV users, enabling "refueling" in under 2 minutes, and lowers the upfront cost of EVs by decoupling the battery from the vehicle.

Draft National EV Charging Guidelines (2025):
- Mandatory fast chargers at all new and existing fuel stations by 2027.
- Preferential tariffs for EV charging during non-peak hours to ease grid stress.
- Capital subsidies for private players setting up residential and commercial charging stations.

PLI 2.0 for Energy Storage (2025):
- Focuses on domestic manufacturing of advanced battery chemistries and ESS to reduce import dependency.

Battery Technology and Domestic Manufacturing Initiatives

The future of India's electric mobility revolution is intrinsically tied to advancements in battery technology and the development of a robust domestic battery manufacturing ecosystem. As electric vehicles (EVs) become mainstream, innovations in batteries are driving down costs, improving performance, and strengthening energy security by reducing reliance on imports.

- **Lithium-Ion Battery Costs:** By March 2025, the cost of lithium-ion batteries in India dropped further to USD 88 per kWh, down from USD 100 per kWh in 2024 and USD 135 per kWh in 2021. This price decline, driven by both global supply chain efficiencies and local manufacturing, is a major factor in making EVs increasingly affordable for Indian consumers.

- **Solid-State Batteries:** Solid-state battery research has made significant strides, with commercialization expected by 2027. These batteries offer higher energy density, longer life, and improved safety.

- **Battery Recycling:** The growth of EVs has underscored the importance of battery recycling to recover critical materials like lithium, cobalt, and nickel, and minimize environmental impact. India's battery recycling capacity has expanded to 32,000 tonnes annually (up from 20,000 tonnes in 2024). Under the Extended Producer Responsibility (EPR) guidelines, EV manufacturers are now mandated to ensure safe collection, recycling, and disposal of spent batteries.

- **Domestic Manufacturing Initiatives:** The Production-Linked Incentive (PLI) scheme for Advanced Chemistry Cell (ACC) battery manufacturing, with an outlay of ₹18,000 crore (USD 2.2 billion), has incentivized local production. By 2024, India's domestic battery manufacturing capacity had reached 5 GWh per year, with plans to expand to 50 GWh by 2030.

PLI Scheme for ACC Batteries:
- Encourages large-scale domestic manufacturing of batteries to cut down on imports and make EVs more cost-competitive.

Battery Waste Management Rules (2022):
- Enforces stringent EPR guidelines for safe disposal and recycling of EV batteries, positioning India as a leader in sustainable battery lifecycle management.

Draft National Battery Storage Policy (2025):
- Proposes tax breaks for investments in battery recycling plants and advanced chemistry cell technologies.
- Targets 100% "Made-in-India" batteries for EVs by 2035.

Battery Management Systems: Ensuring Safety and Performance

A critical yet often overlooked component in electric vehicles is the Battery Management System (BMS). As EV adoption grows, BMS technology ensures battery safety, longevity, and optimal performance.

India has introduced **AIS-156 safety standards** for EV batteries, mandating advanced BMS with features like cell-level monitoring, thermal management, and fault detection.

Domestic companies such as Exicom Tele-Systems, Maxwell Energy, Webber ElectroCorp are innovating in this space. A robust BMS ecosystem is also crucial for India's vision of battery swapping interoperability, ensuring that batteries from different manufacturers can communicate seamlessly with vehicles and chargers.

With the government's focus on standardizing BMS architecture, this area is poised to become a cornerstone of India's EV ecosystem.

Economic and Policy Support for EV Adoption

India's electric vehicle (EV) revolution has been propelled by a strong mix of government policies, tax incentives, and financial support mechanisms designed to make EVs affordable and accelerate their adoption. As EV sales surge across the country, this support continues to play a pivotal role in shaping consumer behavior, encouraging local manufacturing, and developing the supporting ecosystem.

Taxation Incentives and Affordability Boosts

GST Reduction
The Goods and Services Tax (GST) on EVs continues at a concessional rate of 5%, compared to 28% for internal combustion engine (ICE) vehicles. This tax relief has significantly reduced the upfront cost of EVs, making them more appealing to a wider range of consumers.

Income Tax Benefits
Under Section 80EEB of the Income Tax Act, individuals purchasing EVs can claim an additional deduction of up to ₹1.5 lakh on the interest paid for EV loans.

Customs Duty Exemptions (2025):
The government has extended customs duty exemptions for critical EV components such as battery cells, motors, and controllers to support domestic assembly and reduce prices.

PM e-Bus Sewa Scheme: Electrifying Public Transport

In August 2023, the government launched the ambitious PM e-Bus Sewa Scheme, aimed at deploying 10,000 electric buses across 169 cities under a Public Private Partnership (PPP) model. This initiative seeks to:

- Enhance urban mobility in tier-2 and tier-3 cities.
- Promote energy-efficient mass transit.
- Create employment opportunities in EV operations and maintenance.

The scheme provides viability gap funding (VGF) to make electric buses cost-competitive with diesel alternatives.

This effort complements India's goals under the National Electric Bus Programme (NEBP) and reinforces the role of EVs in decarbonizing urban transport.

Image credit: Urban Transport News

EVs as a Component of India's Smart Grid and Renewable Energy Integration

Electric vehicles (EVs) are no longer just a clean transportation solution—they are becoming a vital part of India's evolving smart grid and renewable energy ecosystem, offering grid flexibility, energy storage capabilities, and pathways to decarbonize the power sector.

Vehicle-to-Grid (V2G) Technology:
As of March 2025, India's first set of pilot Vehicle-to-Grid (V2G) projects has gained traction in cities like Gurugram, Bengaluru, and Pune. These projects allow EVs to feed electricity back into the grid during peak demand periods, enabling a bi-directional energy flow that supports:

- Grid balancing during renewable energy fluctuations.

- Enhanced energy storage capacity without requiring massive infrastructure investments.

- Tata Power and MG Motor have partnered on India's first residential V2G program, enabling homeowners with EVs to monetize surplus battery capacity by selling power back to the grid.

- By 2025, over 10,000 EVs are V2G-enabled, with government targets to scale this to 500,000 vehicles by 2030.

Renewable Energy Integration: EVs as Storage Assets
India's renewable energy capacity continues to grow, reaching 44% of total installed power capacity by March 2025. However, the intermittent nature of solar and wind energy requires smart solutions to store and distribute power efficiently.

EVs, with their distributed battery storage, act as mobile energy storage units that can:
- Absorb surplus renewable energy during periods of high generation (e.g., daytime solar peaks).
- Supply power back to the grid or homes during high demand or low renewable generation periods.

This synergy between EVs and renewables is key to India's Net Zero by 2070 roadmap.

Smart charging technologies have been deployed across 40+ Indian cities as of 2025.

These advanced chargers can:
- Adjust charging speeds based on grid load and real-time renewable energy availability.
- Enable time-of-use pricing, encouraging EV owners to charge during off-peak hours or when surplus renewable energy is available.

Examples:
- Bengaluru's Smart Grid Pilot integrates EV chargers with rooftop solar systems, prioritizing clean energy charging.
- Delhi NCR's public charging hubs now include AI-powered load management systems to prevent grid overloading during peak hours.

EV Innovators:
- Tata Motors, Mahindra & Mahindra, and startups like Ola Electric, Ather Energy, and Simple Energy are pushing affordable EVs designed for India's diverse consumer base.
- Ola Electric's Gigafactory in Tamil Nadu now produces batteries optimized for V2G and smart grid applications.

Hydrogen Energy Leadership:
While EVs dominate short- and medium-distance mobility, companies like Reliance Industries, Adani Green Energy, and Indian Oil Corporation are advancing green hydrogen production and distribution to power heavy-duty transport and industrial applications.

After working tirelessly throughout the day, Ankit and Arun finally wrapped up Chapter 9 of the book. As they sat in the quiet office, Ankit leaned back in his chair, a sense of accomplishment washing over him. Arun, with his tablet in hand, was going through the final draft one last time.

You know, Ankit, I think this chapter turned out really well," Arun said, looking up from his screen. "The way we've highlighted the critical role of EVs in reducing fossil fuel dependence, and how they're becoming such a vital part of the renewable energy ecosystem—it's all pretty powerful.

Ankit nodded, satisfied. Yeah, and I think bringing in the data on the rapid expansion of charging stations and battery swapping was key. It shows how the infrastructure is catching up with the rise in EVs.

Arun added, Not to mention how we've linked this to the energy storage solutions and grid stability. The National Energy Storage Mission and V2G technology—these are the future of energy security.

Ankit chuckled. It's funny, you know? Just a few years ago, EVs were seen as a niche market. Now they're becoming the cornerstone of India's energy transition. The government incentives, the policy support—it's all pushing the country in the right direction.

As the conversation continued, they both reflected on how far the industry had come and how the chapter captured the depth of these developments.

Do you think we've covered everything? Ankit asked.

"I'd say so," Arun replied confidently. "We've touched on the FAME II extension, battery technology advancements, domestic manufacturing incentives, and even the role of EVs in enhancing grid flexibility. This chapter is comprehensive. Readers are going to walk away understanding just how integral EVs are to India's energy future.

Ankit smiled, clearly pleased. Let's call it a wrap then. We've built a solid narrative here, one that really ties EVs into the larger story of energy security.

India's electric vehicle revolution is no longer confined to roads and charging stations it is now woven into the very fabric of the country's energy security strategy. EVs have emerged as more than just a cleaner alternative to internal combustion engines; they are energy storage assets, grid stabilizers, and enablers of a decentralized, renewable-powered future.

As of 2025, the rapid growth of EVs, supported by cutting-edge battery technologies, intelligent charging infrastructure, and innovative policy frameworks, has helped India take giant strides toward reducing its dependence on imported oil and lowering carbon emissions.

The integration of Vehicle-to-Grid (V2G) technology and smart grids is transforming EVs into active contributors to energy ecosystems, unlocking new possibilities for renewable energy optimization and grid flexibility.

However, this journey is not without its challenges. Building a resilient EV ecosystem requires continuous focus on domestic battery manufacturing, critical mineral supply chains, and policy alignment across central and state governments. Moreover, consumer awareness and affordability will remain crucial in shaping the pace and inclusivity of EV adoption.

With visionary leadership, bold investments, and collaborative innovation, India is not just creating a market for electric vehicles it is laying the foundation for an energy-independent and climate-resilient future.

As EVs continue to redefine mobility and energy systems, they stand as a testament to India's ability to turn challenges into opportunities and become a global leader in sustainable transportation and clean energy integration.

Chapter 10: Green Hydrogen, the fuel of future

- Introduction to Green Hydrogen and Its Importance for India's Energy Security

- India's Green Hydrogen Roadmap: Policies and Initiatives

- Green Hydrogen Production: Technologies and Infrastructure Development

- Green Hydrogen's Role in Decarbonizing Key Sectors

- Storage and Transportation Challenges of Green Hydrogen

- Economic Viability and Cost Reduction Pathways for Green Hydrogen

- Global Partnerships in Advancing India's Green Hydrogen Sector

Ankit sat at his desk, scrolling through the initial draft of the chapter on green hydrogen. His brow furrowed in concentration as he reviewed the details about India's National Hydrogen Mission and the ambitious plans of major players like Reliance and Adani.

Just then, his phone buzzed with a video call from Dr. Charusmita.

Ankit: Charu! Perfect timing. I was just thinking about you while working on this green hydrogen chapter."

Dr. Charusmita: Thinking about me? That sounds serious. What's going on?

Ankit: Well, I've been putting together this chapter on green hydrogen for my book, and honestly, it feel massive. It's not just about electrolysis or storage it's about building an entire ecosystem: policies, infrastructure, global trade partnerships. And I realized there's no way I can do justice to it without your input.

Dr. Charusmita: You're talking about my favorite topic. I'm already intrigued. Tell me more—how are you approaching it?

Ankit: So far, I've tried to cover the National Hydrogen Mission, the production technologies—alkaline electrolysis, PEM, solid oxide—and the infrastructure challenges. I've even started mapping companies like Reliance and Adani for their mega plans, and Statcon Energiaa for rectifiers. But I feel like I'm missing depth in the technical and policy integration parts. That's where I hoped you'd come in.

Dr. Charusmita: You're pulling me into dangerous territory, Ankit. You know how I can go on and on about hydrogen.

Ankit: Exactly why I need you! This chapter can't just skim the surface; it needs the perspective of someone who's seen how technology, policy, and infrastructure align—or fail to align—in real life.

Dr. Charusmita: Alright then, let's dive deep. First, we'll strengthen the section on production technologies. I'll help you frame the pros and cons of alkaline vs PEM vs SOEC and map them to what's happening in India. And storage— you're covering ammonia-based solutions and LOHCs too, right?

Ankit: Yes, but I've only got the basics. I figured you'd help me make it more practical and forward-looking.

Dr. Charusmita: Good call. We'll also need to bring in renewable energy integration and maybe even touch on India's export potential. And don't forget partnerships with Germany, Japan, and Australia—they're key to India's global strategy.

Ankit: That's exactly the kind of insight I was hoping for. Honestly, Charu, if you're in, this will go from being a good chapter to a phenomenal one.

Dr. Charusmita: I'm in. Let's build this together. Green hydrogen isn't just a topic for me—it's the story of India's clean energy future. And if we tell it right, this chapter will be the heartbeat of your book.

Ankit: Deal. Get ready for a lot of calls, texts, and brainstorming sessions."
Dr. Charusmita: "Bring it on. Let's make this the chapter that everyone remembers

Introduction to Green Hydrogen and Its Importance for India's Energy Security

Green hydrogen, produced by splitting water into hydrogen and oxygen using renewable energy sources such as solar and wind, is emerging as a **cornerstone of India's clean energy transition.**

Unlike gray hydrogen, which relies on fossil fuels, and blue hydrogen, which captures and stores CO_2 emissions during production, **green hydrogen is entirely emissions-free**, offering a pathway to deep decarbonization across sectors.

For India, a country that imports nearly **85% of its crude oil** and 55% of its natural gas needs, green hydrogen represents more than just a clean fuel—it is a strategic tool for achieving energy independence. Its importance lies in its versatility and ability to serve as a clean substitute in industries and sectors traditionally hard to decarbonize.

Decarbonizing Heavy Industry

- Green hydrogen can replace coking coal and natural gas in industries such as **steel, cement, and chemicals**, which collectively account for over **25% of India's CO_2 emissions**.

- Pilots like the **Hydrogen-based Direct Reduced Iron (H-DRI)** process in the steel sector are already underway in India.

Fuel for Heavy Transport

- In long-haul applications like **trucks, trains, ships, and even aviation**, green hydrogen or hydrogen-derived fuels (like ammonia) offer a viable alternative to fossil fuels.

- Indian Railways has begun trials of **hydrogen-powered trains**, aiming to phase out diesel locomotives by 2035.

Energy Storage and Grid Balancing

As renewable energy forms a larger share of India's electricity mix (reaching **44% of total capacity by March 2025**), green hydrogen can serve as a seasonal energy storage solution, helping balance the intermittency of wind and solar power.

India's Green Hydrogen Roadmap: Policies and Initiatives

In **January 2023**, the Government of India formally launched the **National Green Hydrogen Mission (NGHM)**—a bold, future-focused initiative to position India as a global leader in the production, consumption, and export of green hydrogen.

This mission represents a significant step in India's journey toward energy security, economic resilience, and climate leadership.

Key Objectives of the National Green Hydrogen Mission

Production Targets

- Achieve 5 million tonnes (5 MTPA) of green hydrogen production capacity annually by 2030, with a roadmap to scale to 10 MTPA by 2040.

- Create associated renewable energy capacity of 125 GW dedicated to green hydrogen production by 2030.

R&D and Innovation

- Prioritize **research and development** into cost-effective electrolyzer technologies (PEM, alkaline, and solid oxide).

- Encourage innovation in **storage, transport solutions**, and utilization pathways such as hydrogen blending in natural gas pipelines.

Incentives and Infrastructure

- Financial incentives for hydrogen production and manufacturing of electrolyzers under the **Strategic Interventions for Green Hydrogen Transition (SIGHT)** program.

- Support for developing **green hydrogen** hubs in renewable-rich states like Gujarat, Rajasthan, and Tamil Nadu.

Global Trade and Partnerships

Establish India as a hub for **hydrogen exports**, with strategic partnerships being developed with countries like **Japan, Germany**, and **Australia** to supply green hydrogen and ammonia.

Policy Milestones as of March 31, 2025

Hydrogen Production Incentives

- Up to **₹50/kg (USD 0.60/kg)** subsidy for green hydrogen producers under NGHM Phase I.

- Targeted support for industries using green hydrogen, such as fertilizers, refining, and steel production.

Renewable Energy Tariff Concessions

- Reduced tariffs and priority grid access for renewable energy used in green hydrogen production.

Electrolyzer Manufacturing Push

- Under the PLI Scheme for Advanced Chemistry Cells (ACC) and electrolyzers, India's electrolyzer manufacturing capacity has reached 20 GW/year, aiming for 50 GW/year by 2030.

Pilot Projects and Demonstrations

- Indian Oil Corporation (IOC) has commissioned India's first green hydrogen plant at Mathura Refinery (15 MW electrolyzer capacity).

- NTPC's 50 MW green hydrogen plant in Gujarat is now operational.

Private Sector Leadership

Developing the world's largest green energy complex in Jamnagar, Gujarat, with a target of producing 1 MTPA green hydrogen by 2030. The facility will include integrated renewable energy, electrolyzer manufacturing, and hydrogen-based fuels like ammonia and methanol.

Focused on building a 1 MTPA green hydrogen capacity, with plans for export infrastructure to supply green ammonia to markets in Europe and Asia.

IndianOil

Incorporating green hydrogen into refinery operations to replace fossil-based hydrogen. IOC's Mathura Refinery now hosts India's first large-scale green hydrogen plant (15 MW electrolyzer capacity).

In joint ventures to set up electrolyzer manufacturing plants and deploy renewable-to-hydrogen projects for industrial use.

- Tata Motors is experimenting with hydrogen fuel-cell-powered buses and trucks for heavy-duty transport.
- Tata Power is investing in electrolyzer manufacturing and exploring hydrogen blending in natural gas pipelines.
- The group is also working on hydrogen applications for steel production through Tata Steel's R&D efforts.

Green Hydrogen Production: Technologies and Infrastructure Development

India is at the forefront of building a robust green hydrogen ecosystem, with its installed electrolysis capacity reaching **850 MW as of March 31, 2025**, a significant jump from 500 MW a year ago.

This growth is being driven by rapid technological advancements, strategic partnerships, and government-backed initiatives under the National Green Hydrogen Mission. The deployment of cutting-edge electrolysis technologies is critical for scaling up production and achieving cost competitiveness in the global market.

Alkaline Electrolysis:

Alkaline electrolysis is one of the most established and cost-effective methods for green hydrogen production. It uses a liquid alkaline solution (potassium or sodium hydroxide) to conduct electrolysis and is a scalable technology.

- Companies Working in India:
  - **Tata Projects:** Tata Projects is collaborating with global technology leaders to deploy large-scale alkaline electrolyzers in renewable energy hubs such as Gujarat and Rajasthan.

  - **L&T (Larsen & Toubro):** L&T has entered the green hydrogen space with a focus on installing and scaling up alkaline electrolyzers, as part of their larger investment in renewable energy infrastructure.

Proton Exchange Membrane (PEM) Electrolysis:

PEM electrolysis is a newer, more efficient technology that operates at higher current densities and is well-suited to renewable energy integration. PEM electrolyzers are ideal for decentralized production due to their flexibility and responsiveness to intermittent renewable power.

- Companies Working in India:
    - **Cummins India:** Cummins, through its subsidiary Hydrogenics, is supplying PEM electrolyzers to green hydrogen projects in India. It is working with both public and private partners to establish small and medium-sized hydrogen production units across the country.

    - **Reliance Industries:** Reliance has announced significant investments in PEM electrolyzers, aiming to develop high-efficiency hydrogen production plants linked to its large solar farms in Gujarat.

Solid Oxide Electrolysis (SOEC):

SOEC technology, though still in the research and pilot stages, offers the potential for higher efficiency and lower operational costs in the long run. It operates at high temperatures, which allows for better energy conversion rates.

- Companies Working in India:
    - **Thermax:** Thermax, an Indian energy and environment solutions company, is working on the development of solid oxide electrolyzers in collaboration with international partners. They are focusing on pilot projects to test the scalability of this technology in India.

    - **Bloom Energy (India Operations):** Bloom Energy, known for its solid oxide fuel cells, has been involved in green hydrogen production trials using SOEC technology in India. They are working on high-efficiency solutions for industrial hydrogen production.

Infrastructure Development for Green Hydrogen Production:

Rectifiers and power conversion systems are critical components in green hydrogen production, serving as the link between renewable energy sources and electrolyzers.

These systems convert the Alternating Current (AC) generated by solar and wind farms into Direct Current (DC), which is essential for the electrolysis process. Efficient rectification not only minimizes energy losses but also improves the economics and reliability of green hydrogen production.

As India accelerates its renewable energy and hydrogen integration, the demand for high-performance rectifiers and grid integration technologies is growing exponentially.

Rectifiers and Power Conversion Systems:

Rectifiers convert AC (Alternating Current) from renewable energy sources into DC (Direct Current) required for electrolysis. Efficient rectification is essential for reducing energy losses and improving the overall economics of green hydrogen production.

ABB India:
- ABB is at the forefront of supplying advanced rectifiers and power conversion solutions tailored for large-scale green hydrogen projects.

- They are working closely with Indian developers to integrate their high-efficiency rectifiers into renewable energy-driven hydrogen plants across Gujarat, Tamil Nadu, and Karnataka.

- ABB's solutions support dynamic renewable energy profiles, ensuring consistent DC supply for electrolyzers even during fluctuating solar or wind generation.

Hitachi Energy (India Operations)
- Hitachi Energy is delivering rectifiers, transformers, and energy management systems optimized for hydrogen production facilities.

- Their partnerships with Indian energy giants are focused on grid stabilization and ensuring renewable energy is utilized to its fullest potential during hydrogen generation.

BHEL (Bharat Heavy Electricals Limited)
- BHEL is actively developing rectifiers and power conversion systems customized for green hydrogen electrolysis plants.

- The company is collaborating with public sector oil and gas companies like Indian Oil Corporation and NTPC on pilot projects that combine renewable energy, electrolysis, and advanced power electronics.

Green hydrogen production requires much more than electrolyzers alone. A robust supporting infrastructure is essential to ensure seamless integration of renewable power with hydrogen systems, including:

- **Rectifiers and Transformers:** To convert and stabilize power from renewable sources.
- **Grid Integration Systems:** To manage intermittency and optimize renewable energy utilization.
- **Hydrogen Storage and Transport Solutions:** To safely store and move hydrogen from production sites to consumption hubs.

These components are being developed in tandem with India's **Green Hydrogen Hubs** initiative in renewable-rich states such as Rajasthan, Gujarat, and Tamil Nadu, positioning India to meet its ambitious 5 MTPA green hydrogen target by 2030.

Renewable Energy Integration and Grid Connectivity:

Integrating **large-scale renewable energy projects** with **hydrogen production** facilities is emerging as a cornerstone of India's green hydrogen strategy. The ability to provide a **continuous, reliable, and affordable supply of electricity** to electrolyzers is essential to drive down production costs and achieve scale.

Companies leading India's renewable energy revolution are now playing a pivotal role in ensuring this integration. **ReNew Power**, one of India's largest renewable energy developers, has been investing heavily in dedicated wind and solar farms designed specifically to power hydrogen production facilities.

By **March 2025**, ReNew commissioned over 2 GW of renewable capacity connected to green hydrogen plants under development in Gujarat and Rajasthan. These initiatives mark the creation of India's first renewable-to-hydrogen ecosystems.

Similarly, **Tata Power Sola**r has been deploying utility-scale solar installations across renewable-rich states, supplying clean energy to hydrogen electrolysis units in partnership with both public and private sector entities.

The **Adani Group**, through its renewable energy arm, is also **building hybrid wind-solar parks in Gujarat's Kutch** region, which are being **integrated with large-scale hydrogen and ammonia plants** to support both domestic use and exports.

Hydrogen Storage and Transportation Infrastructure:

Efficient **storage and transportation systems** are equally critical for scaling up green hydrogen production and enabling its deployment across industries and transportation.

Green hydrogen is currently stored in India using **compressed gas systems**; however, new methods such as **liquefied hydrogen** and chemical carriers like **ammonia (NH$_3$)** and **Liquid Organic Hydrogen Carriers (LOHCs)** are being explored to facilitate long-distance transportation and export.

Indian Oil Corporation (IOC) has emerged as a key player in this space, piloting projects that focus on compressed hydrogen storage systems and ammonia-based storage solutions for shipping hydrogen over long distances.

The Adani Group is investing in **hydrogen pipelines** and **refueling stations**, aiming to create a nationwide transport network that connects production hubs with industrial clusters.

Meanwhile, **GAIL (India)** Limited is **experimenting** with **hydrogen blending** in natural gas pipelines as a transitional strategy while simultaneously developing dedicated hydrogen pipelines and storage depots.

Current Challenges and Goals:

The **cost of electrolysis** remains a significant barrier to widespread adoption. As of **March 2025**, the cost of producing green hydrogen in India has dropped to **USD 2.7–3.2 per kg** from **USD 3–4** a year ago, thanks to improvements in electrolyzer efficiency and scaling up of renewable energy projects.

However, achieving the government's ambitious **target of USD 1.5 per kg by 2030** will require continuous technological innovation, further renewable energy expansion, and economies of scale.

India's renewable energy capacity, which reached 175 GW by March 2025, provides a solid foundation for scaling green hydrogen production. But further expansion—especially in states like Gujarat, Rajasthan, and Tamil Nadu—will be necessary to meet the rising demand for green hydrogen across industries and transportation.

Green Hydrogen's Role in Decarbonizing Key Sectors

Green hydrogen plays a critical role in decarbonizing sectors that are challenging to electrify or decarbonize through other means:

- Heavy Industry: Industries like steel, cement, and chemicals are energy-intensive and heavily reliant on fossil fuels. Green hydrogen can replace coal and natural gas in these industries. The Indian government is encouraging pilot projects for using hydrogen in steel manufacturing under its Green Steel Initiative.

- Heavy Transport: In heavy transport, green hydrogen and hydrogen fuel cells provide efficient and scalable solutions for long-haul trucks, intercity buses, trains, and even ships. These segments often face challenges with battery-electric technologies due to range limitations and heavy energy demands. By March 2025, pilot fleets of hydrogen fuel cell buses had already been deployed in cities like Bengaluru and Chennai, showcasing the potential of hydrogen-powered mobility in India's urban and intercity transport networks.

- Ammonia Production: Hydrogen is also a key input for producing ammonia, a critical component of fertilizers. Using green hydrogen for ammonia production could help decarbonize India's agricultural sector.

By integrating hydrogen into these sectors, India can significantly reduce its CO_2 emissions and achieve its Nationally Determined Contributions (NDCs) under the Paris Agreement.

Storage and Transportation Challenges of Green Hydrogen

Hydrogen's low energy density continues to pose significant challenges for its storage and transportation. However, as of March 2025, India has accelerated its research, investments, and pilot programs to overcome these barriers and build a robust hydrogen infrastructure.

- Compressed Hydrogen: Compressed Hydrogen remains one of the primary methods of storage, where hydrogen is stored as a gas at very high pressures—often up to 700 bar. While this method is relatively mature, it is energy-intensive and expensive due to the need for specialized high-pressure tanks and compressors.

- Liquid Hydrogen: Liquid Hydrogen offers a higher energy density solution by storing hydrogen in liquid form at cryogenic temperatures of -253°C. While this method allows for larger quantities of hydrogen to be stored and transported, it demands substantial energy input for liquefaction and highly insulated storage systems to prevent boil-off losses.

- Ammonia-based Storage: Ammonia-based Storage has gained traction as a highly efficient solution. Hydrogen can be converted into ammonia (NH_3) for storage and transportation using existing infrastructure like pipelines and shipping tankers. At the point of use, ammonia can be "cracked" back into hydrogen, making this method ideal for long-distance transport and export.

- Liquid Organic Hydrogen Carriers (LOHCs): Liquid Organic Hydrogen Carriers (LOHCs) are emerging as another promising technology. LOHCs chemically bind hydrogen in a liquid medium that can be transported under ambient conditions, eliminating the need for high pressures or cryogenic temperatures. This makes LOHCs a safer and potentially more cost-effective solution for distributing hydrogen over medium distances.

The Indian government is also taking major strides in developing hydrogen transport infrastructure. Plans are underway to construct **2,500 km of hydrogen pipelines by 2030**, with **pilot projects already operational in Gujarat and Tamil Nadu**. These pipelines will connect green hydrogen production hubs with industrial consumption centers, creating a national hydrogen grid to facilitate large-scale adoption.

Economic Viability and Cost Reduction Pathways for Green Hydrogen

While green hydrogen offers immense potential for transforming India's energy landscape, its economic viability continues to be a major challenge due to the relatively high production costs compared to fossil-fuel-based alternatives. However, significant progress is being made to close this gap, driven by multiple factors.

- **Advancements in electrolysis technology** are playing a critical role in bringing costs down. Innovations in **Proton Exchange Membrane (PEM) and Solid Oxide Electrolysis (SOEC)** technologies are improving conversion efficiency and reducing the operational costs of hydrogen production plants.

- At the same time, renewable energy costs have continued to decline. **By March 2025, solar power prices** in India have reached **USD 0.028 per kWh**, among the lowest in the world, while **wind power prices** stand at **USD 0.034 per kWh**. This makes renewable electricity the key input for green hydrogen production—more affordable and reliable.

- Scaling up production is further driving cost reductions. Large-scale hydrogen production hubs in states like Gujarat and Rajasthan are benefiting from economies of scale, which reduce the per-unit cost of infrastructure, electrolyzers, and associated systems.

The Indian government has set an ambitious target to lower the cost of green hydrogen from the current range of USD 2.5–3.2 per kg (2025) to USD 1.5 per kg by 2030. Achieving this price parity with fossil-fuel-based hydrogen (gray hydrogen) will be a game-changer, enabling widespread adoption across industrial applications, transportation, and power generation.

If realized, this cost reduction will position India as one of the most competitive players in the global hydrogen economy and significantly accelerate the commercialization of green hydrogen technologies.

Global Partnerships in Advancing India's Green Hydrogen Sector

India is actively collaborating with countries such as Japan, Germany, Australia, and the UAE to develop hydrogen technologies and establish international trade networks.

- In **2025**, India and **Germany** deepened their partnership through the **Indo-German Hydrogen Task Force**, focusing on joint research projects and pilot programs to scale hydrogen production and utilization.

- **Australia** has partnered with India under its **Hydrogen Energy Supply Chain (HESC)** initiative to facilitate green hydrogen exports from India's renewable-rich states to the Asia-Pacific region.

- Discussions with **Japan** have advanced plans for establishing a hydrogen shipping corridor, enabling India to export liquefied green hydrogen to meet Japan's clean energy goals by 2035.

Green hydrogen stands at the forefront of India's clean energy transition, offering a transformative solution to decarbonize hard-to-abate sectors and strengthen energy security. With its ability to fuel industries, power transportation, and serve as a large-scale energy storage medium, green hydrogen is poised to redefine how India produces and consumes energy.

The initiatives under the National Hydrogen Mission, combined with bold investments from public and private players, are laying the foundation for a robust hydrogen ecosystem.

From the development of advanced electrolyzer technologies to innovations in storage and transport infrastructure, every step brings India closer to realizing its target of producing 5 million tonnes of green hydrogen annually by 2030.

However, challenges such as high production costs, infrastructure gaps, and the need for clear regulatory frameworks remain. Overcoming these barriers will require sustained policy support, technological innovation, and strong global and domestic partnerships.

As India accelerates its efforts, green hydrogen has the potential to make the country not just energy secure but energy independent—positioning it as a global leader in the emerging hydrogen economy. The coming decade will determine whether India can seize this opportunity to pioneer a cleaner, more resilient energy future.

Arun: Ankit, I have to say, this chapter on Green Hydrogen feels incredibly comprehensive. The way it moves from technology to policy to India's global ambitions it really ties everything together.

Ankit: Thanks, Arun. I can't take all the credit though. Dr. Charusmita worked with me closely on this one. Her inputs shaped a lot of the narrative and technical depth.

Arun: Oh really? That explains why the section on electrolyzer technologies and hydrogen storage is so detailed. It's rare to see someone weave technical insights with policy developments so seamlessly.

Ankit: Exactly. Charu suggested we structure the production technologies into Alkaline, PEM, and SOEC, and then map them to the companies operating in India. That approach made the content more relatable for readers trying to understand who's doing what in this space.

Arun: I loved the part on partnerships too India's collaborations with Germany, Japan, and Australia and how they could shape our export future. Was that her suggestion as well?

Ankit: Yes, she insisted we shouldn't just focus on domestic initiatives but also highlight India's positioning in the global hydrogen economy. That's why we added the hydrogen shipping corridor with Japan and the Indo-German Hydrogen Task Force details.

Arun: And the cost reduction section? The target to bring hydrogen down to $1.5/kg by 2030 really stood out.

Ankit: That was her idea too. She wanted us to end the chapter with a forward-looking perspective so readers see not just the challenges but also the roadmap to viability.

Arun: Well, the collaboration clearly worked. This chapter feels both technical and accessible.

Ankit: I agree. Charu's expertise in hydrogen technologies really elevated it. I feel like we've built a solid foundation for readers to understand why green hydrogen is the linchpin for India's clean energy future.

Chapter 11: India's Geopolitical Energy Relationships

- Energy Diplomacy with Middle Eastern Countries

- India-Russia Energy Ties: Oil, Gas, and Nuclear Partnerships

- Role of the United States in Supporting India's Clean Energy Transition

- China-India Energy Competition and Cooperation

- India's Energy Relations with ASEAN and African Nations

- India's Role in Global Energy Forums

Arun: Ankit this chapter is going to be one of the most important chapters of this book, I think you should get some external help for this chapter.

Ankit: I know so I already have asked Saswat sir to help me with this chapter and he will be here in some time for the same.

Hearing the name Saswat, Arun smiled and said, its been too long that we have sat with him and have a conversation, I better arrange some snacks.

Saswat Panda, the RE-100 Program Manager at The Climate Group is well known for his commitmment to carbon neutral lifestyle. He is a well informed person about the industry and the global market.

Ankit (leaning forward at the table): Saswat sir, I'm glad you could make it today. We've been deep into this chapter on India's geopolitical energy relationships, and Arun and I both felt it was crucial to get your insights, especially with your experience at The Climate Group. There's so much happening in terms of energy diplomacy.

Arun: Absolutely, Saswat sir. Ankit's got this solid draft going, but I think you could help us fill in a few gaps, especially around how India is positioning itself in energy trading.

Saswat: Thanks for inviting me, guys. It's an exciting time to be discussing this topic, especially with India pushing toward renewable energy while still being heavily reliant on oil and gas imports. I've had some interesting conversations lately about the Middle East and Russia, and their energy influence on India. But before we dive in, what's your main focus with this chapter?

Ankit: We're covering India's key relationships, starting with the Middle East, Russia, and the US. But we're also digging into more complex dynamics with China and exploring ties with ASEAN and African nations. The goal is to show how energy security isn't just about domestic capacity—it's a geopolitical game.

Saswat: That's a strong approach. One thing I'd definitely suggest is expanding on India's role in global energy forums. Platforms like the G20, International Energy Agency (IEA), and BRICS aren't just opportunities for dialogue, they're where policy alignment happens. India's influence has grown significantly, particularly as it becomes one of the largest energy consumers globally.

Ankit: We touched on international cooperation but didn't dive too deeply into those forums. It makes sense to highlight how India is shaping global energy policies.

Saswat: Exactly, and don't forget about multilateral development banks like the World Bank and the Asian Development Bank. They've been crucial in securing financing for India's renewable energy projects, particularly solar and wind. This is a key part of how India is balancing its push for renewables while still needing foreign investments.

Ankit: That's a great point. I didn't emphasize the financing angle enough, especially with how those institutions are driving projects in India. I've got to update that.

Saswat: There's also technological cooperation—India's partnerships in hydrogen tech, carbon capture, and battery storage are big news right now. You've got initiatives with countries like the US and Germany on clean energy technology transfer. It's not just about getting energy anymore, it's about getting the tech that helps us reduce emissions.

Ankit: So, we should broaden the section on partnerships to cover not just energy supplies but also innovation and technology transfers. I can see how it'll strengthen the narrative, especially around renewables and decarbonization.

Ankit: Right. And what about Latin America? We're talking a lot about the Middle East and Russia, but India's looking toward Latin America too, right? Should we mention Venezuela and Brazil in terms of oil imports?

Saswat: Definitely. India's relationships with countries like Brazil and Venezuela are growing, especially for oil. It's part of India's diversification strategy—reducing its dependence on Middle Eastern oil alone.

Arun: This chapter is starting to feel like a comprehensive diplomatic roadmap for energy.

Saswat (smiling): Exactly, that's the idea. Energy security isn't just about oil anymore, it's about how you manage partnerships across the globe, where technology plays as much a role as oil barrels. And don't forget, energy diplomacy is also a balancing act—how India competes and cooperates with China is a story in itself.

India's journey toward energy security is increasingly shaped not just by domestic policies and innovations but also by its intricate web of geopolitical relationships.

As the third-largest energy consumer in the world, India must cultivate strategic energy partnerships to ensure its supply chains remain resilient amid growing demand, volatile global markets, and shifting geopolitical dynamics.

This chapter explores the various international relationships influencing India's energy landscape highlighting its longstanding ties with Middle Eastern nations, its deepening collaboration with Russia, and its strategic clean energy partnerships with the United States.

Given India's dependence on imported fossil fuels particularly crude oil and natural gas energy diplomacy has become a cornerstone of its foreign policy. As of March 2025, over 58% of India's crude oil imports originate from the Middle East, with Iraq, Saudi Arabia, and the UAE remaining key suppliers. India has also diversified its LNG imports with Qatar, Oman, and the UAE playing a growing role in meeting its natural gas needs.

Meanwhile, India's engagement with Russia has expanded beyond oil and gas to include nuclear energy cooperation, Arctic LNG projects, and joint ventures in hydrogen technology. In 2024, India secured long-term contracts for LNG supplies from Russia's Arctic LNG-2 project, ensuring stable gas imports despite global disruptions.

The United States has emerged as a critical partner in India's clean energy transformation, collaborating on solar, wind, hydrogen, and advanced battery storage technologies. Initiatives under the U.S.-India Strategic Clean Energy Partnership (SCEP) have driven joint research, technology transfers, and large-scale renewable energy investments.

India's energy relationship with China remains complex marked by competition in global energy markets and cooperation in renewable energy supply chains. While India depends on China for solar PV components and rare earths, it is also actively seeking to localize manufacturing under the Make in India initiative to reduce over-reliance.

Beyond these major powers, India is also strengthening ties with ASEAN and African nations, focusing on critical minerals (like cobalt and lithium), oil exploration partnerships, and solar energy deployment in energy-deficient regions. These partnerships are crucial for diversifying energy sources and supporting India's long-term energy security goals.

By analyzing India's geopolitical energy strategies and key alliances, this chapter highlights how international relationships will define the country's ability to meet rising energy needs while accelerating its transition to cleaner, sustainable alternatives.

Energy Diplomacy with Middle Eastern Countries

The Middle East, particularly the Gulf Cooperation Council (GCC) countries, continues to be vital for India's energy security, supplying a substantial portion of the country's crude oil and natural gas imports.

India's Dependence on Middle Eastern Oil:

- As of March 2025, nearly 58% of India's crude oil imports came from the Middle East. Iraq, Saudi Arabia, the United Arab Emirates (UAE), and Kuwait remain among India's top suppliers:

- Iraq continues as India's largest oil supplier, accounting for approximately 26% of India's total oil imports in 2024-25.

- Saudi Arabia ranks second, contributing 19% of India's crude imports and serving as a strategic partner in energy infrastructure development.

- UAE has strengthened energy cooperation with India through the Strategic Petroleum Reserve (SPR) agreement. In 2024, the UAE became the first foreign country to store 1.5 million barrels of crude oil in India's SPR facilities in Mangalore, Karnataka.

Natural Gas and LNG Imports:

India is the world's fourth-largest importer of liquefied natural gas (LNG), and the Middle East plays a central role in this trade.
- As of 2024, India imported 32 million tonnes per annum (mtpa) of LNG, with Qatar supplying 13 mtpa, maintaining its position as India's largest LNG supplier.

- India and the UAE signed agreements to enhance cooperation in LNG, focusing on long-term contracts and joint investments in LNG terminals in India's western coast.

India is actively diversifying its energy partnerships within the Middle East to go beyond oil and gas.

- In 2024, India and Saudi Arabia signed a strategic agreement to jointly invest in petrochemical projects and refineries. Saudi Aramco reaffirmed its interest in investing in India's Ratnagiri Refinery and Petrochemical Complex, a USD 44 billion project, expected to become South Asia's largest refinery.

- India is also collaborating with the UAE and Saudi Arabia on renewable energy initiatives, particularly in solar power projects and green hydrogen development. These partnerships align with both regions' shared vision of reducing dependence on fossil fuels and transitioning to cleaner energy systems.

Other Important Collaborations in Middle-East...

Iran:

- **Oil Imports:** Iran has historically been a significant crude oil supplier to India, even during periods of U.S. sanctions. However, since 2019, Indian oil imports from Iran halted due to U.S. sanctions. In 2024, India has resumed discussions with Tehran on the potential revival of oil imports under rupee-based trade agreements, which could bypass dollar-denominated transactions.

- **Chabahar Port:** India's investment in Iran's Chabahar Port remains crucial for establishing a strategic transit route to Central Asia and Afghanistan, bypassing Pakistan. The port also has future potential as a key hub for energy transit pipelines and LNG shipments from Central Asia to India.

Nigeria:

- **Oil and Gas Supplies:** Nigeria continues to be one of India's top suppliers of crude oil and natural gas, providing around 10% of India's total oil imports in 2024. Long-term contracts ensure energy security and reduce overdependence on Middle Eastern suppliers.

- **LNG Cooperation:** India is expanding its footprint in Nigeria's LNG sector through investments and joint ventures. Indian companies are exploring stakes in new LNG trains to secure reliable supplies for India's growing gas demand.

Mozambique:

- **LNG Projects:** India holds significant stakes in Mozambique's Rovuma Basin LNG project, which is expected to supply up to 12 million tonnes per annum (mtpa) of LNG to India. Production is projected to ramp up by late 2025.

- **Energy Investments:** Indian state-owned enterprises such as ONGC Videsh and BPCL have invested over USD 6 billion in Mozambique's offshore gas fields, positioning India as a long-term partner in Africa's LNG supply chain.

India's energy ties with the Middle East remain critical, but notable shifts in geopolitical strategy are underway:

- The formation of new alliances like **I2U2 (India-Israel-UAE-US)** reflects a realignment of India's energy security efforts towards broader cooperation, encompassing technology transfer, trade, and renewable energy collaborations.

- India is also actively pursuing hydrogen and solar partnerships with Gulf countries, signaling a transition from a traditional fossil fuel importer to a diversified energy player.

These developments are helping India strengthen its long-term energy security vision, ensuring resilience beyond crude oil by integrating renewables and fostering technology-driven energy partnerships.

India-Russia Energy Ties: Oil, Gas, and Nuclear Partnerships

India and Russia share a deep and multifaceted energy partnership, covering crude oil, natural gas, nuclear energy, and even defense-related energy collaboration. As India seeks to diversify its energy sources and reduce dependency on any single region, Russia has emerged as a critical partner in this strategy.

Crude Oil Imports from Russia:

In the wake of the Ukraine conflict and Western sanctions on Moscow, India became one of the largest importers of discounted Russian crude oil. As of March 2024, Russia accounted for approximately 22% of India's total crude oil imports, a dramatic rise from less than 2% before 2022.

- India imported an average of 1.7 million barrels per day (bpd) of Russian oil in 2023–24, making it **Russia's second-largest oil market globally** after China.

- The diversification helped India secure lower-cost crude during a period of high global energy price volatility, ensuring domestic price stability.

Natural Gas and LNG Cooperation:

India and Russia are expanding their cooperation in natural gas through long-term agreements and joint projects.

- **Gazprom** and **GAIL (India) Ltd.** maintain a **20-year LNG supply contract**, which continues to be a significant contributor to India's LNG portfolio. In 2023–24, Gazprom supplied 3.5 million tonnes of LNG to India under this agreement.

- Indian companies like **ONGC Videsh** have invested in Russia's **Arctic LNG 2 project**, acquiring stakes to secure long-term gas supplies.

- Discussions are ongoing about setting up LNG regasification terminals in India specifically for Russian LNG cargoes.

India's engagement with Central Asia is also gaining momentum:

- **Oil and Gas Supplies:** Countries like **Kazakhstan**, **Uzbekistan**, and **Turkmenistan** are emerging as energy partners. India has signed agreements for crude oil and gas exploration in Kazakhstan and Uzbekistan.

- **TAPI Gas Pipeline:** The long-discussed **Turkmenistan-Afghanistan-Pakistan-India (TAPI)** gas pipeline remains a vision for importing natural gas from Turkmenistan. However, geopolitical instability in Afghanistan continues to delay its implementation.

- **Nuclear Energy Cooperation:** Kazakhstan, as one of the world's largest uranium producers, supplies uranium to India's civil nuclear program under the **India-Kazakhstan Nuclear Cooperation Agreement.**

Russia remains **India's most important partner in the civil nuclear energy sector:**

- The **Kudankulam Nuclear Power Plant (KNPP)** in Tamil Nadu, constructed with Russian assistance, is a flagship project of this partnership.
  - As of March 2024, two reactors (Units 1 and 2) are operational.
  - Units 3 and 4 are under advanced stages of construction and expected to be commissioned by 2026.
  - Plans for Units 5 and 6 have been approved, with groundwork starting in early 2025.

- Russia has committed to supporting India's broader nuclear energy ambitions by:
  - Providing advanced reactor technologies.
  - Supplying nuclear fuel under long-term agreements.
  - Offering training and technical maintenance for Indian nuclear facilities.

Role of the United States in Supporting India's Clean Energy Transition

The United States has emerged as one of India's most significant partners in accelerating its clean energy transition, offering robust support in renewable energy development, technology transfer, financing, and research collaborations. This partnership has become a cornerstone of India's efforts to achieve its ambitious climate and energy security goals.

US-India Strategic Clean Energy Partnership (SCEP):

The **US-India Strategic Clean Energy Partnership (SCEP)**, relaunched in 2021, has become a key platform for collaboration in energy security, renewable energy, and climate resilience.
- By **March 2024**, SCEP had facilitated USD 5.5 billion in joint projects, spanning solar energy, energy storage, and grid modernization initiatives.

- Agencies such as **USAID** and the **US Department of Energy** have provided technical assistance to integrate 45 GW of solar and wind energy into India's power grid, supporting India's target of 500 GW renewable energy capacity by 2030.

Collaboration in Solar and Wind Energy:

The **US-India Clean Energy Finance Initiative** has successfully mobilized **USD 1.2 billion** in private sector investment for renewable energy projects in India by 2024.

- This initiative has enabled the installation of 5 GW of solar energy capacity, largely through distributed solar rooftop projects in urban and semi-urban areas.

- US companies like First Solar have set up solar module manufacturing facilities in India, strengthening the Make in India campaign and reducing dependency on imports from China.

- Partnerships in offshore wind energy are also gaining traction, with US firms collaborating on projects off the coasts of Tamil Nadu and Gujarat, regions identified as having high offshore wind potential.

Joint Hydrogen and Battery Research:

India and the United States are collaborating closely in advanced energy technologies critical to India's clean energy future:

- The **US-India Hydrogen Task Force**, set up in 2022, is actively working to scale up green hydrogen production in India and build the infrastructure for its distribution. Pilot projects in Gujarat and Rajasthan are underway with US technical inputs.

- Collaborative research in **advanced battery technologies**, such as solid-state batteries and next-generation energy storage systems, is helping India overcome challenges in grid storage and electric mobility.

China-India Energy Competition and Cooperation

The energy relationship between India and China is characterized by a delicate balance of competition and cooperation. As the two largest energy consumers in Asia, both countries are pursuing ambitious strategies to secure energy supplies and transition toward cleaner sources. While competition dominates in global energy markets, collaborative efforts in renewable energy and technology sharing have emerged in recent years.

Energy Competition:

- **Oil and Gas:** India and China remain **fierce competitors** in securing oil and gas supplies from the **Middle East, Africa, and Central Asia**. Both nations actively bid for oil fields and LNG contracts, but **China's larger financial and diplomatic leverage** often gives it an edge. For example, China's investments in African oil fields and LNG terminals in Mozambique have outpaced India's efforts in the region.

- **Geopolitical Competition: China's Belt and Road Initiative (BRI)**, which includes significant energy infrastructure projects in South Asia and the Indian Ocean, continues to raise concerns in India. Projects like the **China-Pakistan Economic Corridor (CPEC)** and Chinese-built ports in Sri Lanka are viewed as potential threats to India's regional energy security.

Areas of Cooperation:

- **Renewable Energy:** Despite competition, China and India are closely linked in the renewable energy supply chain. India imports **nearly 78% of its solar panels and key components** from China due to cost advantages, even as India seeks to ramp up domestic manufacturing under the **PLI (Production-Linked Incentive)** scheme.

- **Bilateral Dialogues:** Both countries have engaged in **BRICS energy forums** and Asian Infrastructure Investment Bank (AIIB) meetings to discuss shared energy challenges.

- **Technology Collaboration:** In 2023, India and China initiated dialogues on energy efficiency and grid modernization. Chinese companies have provided smart grid technologies and battery storage solutions for pilot projects in India, especially in urban areas and renewable energy parks.

India's Energy Relations with ASEAN and African Nations

India has been steadily expanding its energy relationships with ASEAN and African nations to diversify energy sources and strengthen economic ties with resource-rich regions. These partnerships align with India's strategy of reducing dependence on the Middle East and exploring new markets for both hydrocarbons and renewable energy.

ASEAN Energy Relations:

India is working closely with **ASEAN countries**, particularly **Indonesia, Malaysia, and Vietnam**, to secure access to oil and gas resources. As of March 2024, ONGC Videsh continues to hold stakes in several offshore oil blocks in Vietnam, reinforcing India's presence in Southeast Asia's hydrocarbon sector.

India is also scaling up investments in renewable energy projects in ASEAN, focusing on **solar partnerships** with **Thailand** and the **Philippines**, and exploring offshore wind potential in Vietnam. These initiatives complement **India's Act East Policy**, which seeks to deepen economic and energy ties with Southeast Asia.

At the India-ASEAN Energy Ministers' Meeting (2023), key agreements were signed to strengthen cooperation in LNG trade, renewable energy development, and regional energy security frameworks.

India-Singapore and India-Australia Energy Trading via Singapore

Singapore plays a pivotal role in India's energy trade as a global hub for **LNG** and **refined petroleum products**. India engages with Singapore for:
- **LNG re-exports** and the trading of oil products.
- Leveraging Singapore's financial and logistical infrastructure for energy pricing, hedging mechanisms, and energy financing.

Additionally, India's growing energy partnership with Australia—particularly in LNG and critical minerals for battery manufacturing—often flows through Singapore's trading systems, reinforcing the island nation's role as a gateway for India's global energy trade.

South Korea:
- **Technology Collaboration:** South Korea remains pivotal in enabling technology transfer for smart grids, battery storage systems, and renewable energy technologies. Korean firms like Hyundai Heavy Industries and LG Energy Solution have partnered with Indian companies to develop advanced solar, wind, and energy storage projects in states such as Tamil Nadu and Maharashtra.

- **Energy Investments:** South Korean energy companies are expanding their footprint in India's renewable energy landscape. Discussions are ongoing for LNG supply agreements and collaborations in green hydrogen technologies, signaling a broader energy technology partnership.

Japan:
- **Energy Technology Partnerships:** Japan is a critical partner in India's clean energy transition, supporting projects in green hydrogen, carbon capture utilization and storage (CCUS), and energy efficiency upgrades. The two countries are co-developing pilot hydrogen projects under the Japan-India Clean Energy Cooperation Framework.

- **LNG Trade:** As a global LNG leader, Japan continues discussions with India on long-term LNG supply contracts and technology sharing for LNG regasification terminals.

- **Strategic Energy Cooperation:** The Japan-India Energy Dialogue has strengthened bilateral cooperation on nuclear energy (for civil use), renewable energy grid integration, and financing mechanisms, with Japan providing concessional loans for renewable infrastructure projects.

Indonesia:

- **Coal Imports:** Indonesia remains India's largest supplier of thermal coal, meeting over 40% of India's coal import demand in 2023-24. This trade supports India's thermal power plants, which still account for nearly 50% of total electricity generation.

- **Energy Geopolitics:** Given Indonesia's proximity and vast energy reserves, it plays a strategic role in India's Act East Policy, which emphasizes energy security and trade diversification.

Country	Energy Trade	Technology Transfer	Strategic Initiatives
South Korea	Discussions on LNG imports, investment in renewable energy projects, and partnerships in battery storage systems.	Smart grids, advanced battery technologies, renewable energy systems, and potential hydrogen technology	Expanding investment footprint in India's renewable energy sector and Act East energy collaboration.
Japan	Long-term LNG supply talks; supports India's LNG terminal technology and nuclear energy collaboration.	Hydrogen energy projects, carbon capture utilization and storage (CCUS), and energy efficiency technologies.	Japan-India Energy Dialogue, clean energy cooperation framework, and concessional financing for renewable projects.
Indonesia	India's largest thermal coal supplier; 40% of coal imports come from Indonesia; also exploring renewables cooperation.	Renewable energy cooperation discussions (offshore wind, bioenergy), limited technology transfer compared to Korea and Japan.	Part of India's Act East Policy; vital for energy security through coal trade and emerging renewables focus.

India's Role in Global Energy Forums

India's growing energy needs and its commitment to sustainability have positioned it as a key player in shaping global energy dialogues. Active participation in international forums such as the **International Energy Agency (IEA), G20 Energy Transitions Working Group**, and **BRICS Energy** Dialogues underscores India's efforts to influence global energy policies while addressing its domestic priorities.

At the **IEA**, where India has held "Association Country" status since 2017, it continues to advocate for equitable energy transition frameworks that account for the unique challenges of emerging economies.

In 2024, India and the IEA launched a **joint roadmap for bioenergy and energy efficiency**, emphasizing affordable clean energy access for developing nations.

During the **G20 Energy Meetings**, India leveraged its G20 presidency in 2023 to introduce initiatives such as the **Global Biofuels Alliance**, aiming to scale biofuel adoption worldwide. India also advocated for improved energy equity, calling for increased financial flows to support renewable energy deployment in the Global South.

In the **BRICS Energy Forums**, India focuses on fostering south-south cooperation. Recent collaborations have included knowledge sharing on smart grids, hydrogen technology, and offshore wind energy projects, with a goal to align energy security needs with climate action.

Through these platforms, India continues to promote its vision of a just, inclusive, and sustainable global energy transition, cementing its role as a leader among developing nations navigating the energy-climate nexus.

India's geopolitical energy relationships are pivotal in shaping its path to long-term energy security and sustainability. From its crude oil and natural gas dependencies in the Middle East and Russia to cutting-edge collaborations in clean energy technologies with the United States, India's international energy strategy has evolved into a dynamic and forward-looking framework.

The country's growing engagement in **green hydrogen development, renewable energy partnerships**, and nuclear cooperation highlights its commitment to aligning energy security with climate goals.

At the same time, strategic ties with ASEAN and African nations are enabling India to diversify its energy imports and reduce overreliance on any single region.

As of **March 31, 2024**, India's energy diplomacy reflects a deliberate effort to balance immediate fossil fuel requirements with the global shift towards sustainable energy systems. This multifaceted approach not only strengthens India's resilience to global energy market fluctuations but also positions the country as a proactive player in the world's energy transition.

Ankit: Saswat sir, thanks again for coming through today. We've finally wrapped up the chapter on India's geopolitical energy relationships. It's been a complex one—covering everything from oil diplomacy to clean energy partnerships.

Arun (scrolling through the final draft): Yeah, there's a lot to absorb here. What really stands out for me is how intertwined India's energy security is with its global partnerships. I hadn't fully realized how much of our future depends on maintaining relationships with countries like Russia, the US, and even China—each for different reasons.

Saswat (smiling): That's the key takeaway, Arun. Energy diplomacy is no longer just about securing oil barrels. It's about strategic partnerships, technology transfers, and balancing foreign investments. And India is in a unique position—it's shaping global energy policy while still ensuring domestic security.

Arun: I hadn't considered the role of multilateral development banks like the World Bank and ADB. They've played such a huge role in funding India's renewable energy projects, and we're now at a point where these collaborations are the foundation of our future energy security.

Ankit: Absolutely. I've added a section on India's growing influence in global energy forums like the G20 and BRICS, but you're right—there's an economic and technology aspect we need to highlight more. The funding, the innovations, the hydrogen initiatives—it's all part of the same story.

Saswat: And that's the future of energy diplomacy—countries that can collaborate on clean energy tech, like hydrogen and battery storage, will dominate the next few decades. India's partnerships with the US and Germany are critical for our long-term energy independence.

Chapter 12: Roadmap for the Future: Vision 2044

- India's Long-term Energy Strategy: Policies and Goals

- The Role of Innovation in Achieving Energy Security

- Public-Private Collaboration for Sustainable Energy Development

- Socio-Economic Impacts of India's Energy Transition

- A Sustainable Energy Future: Challenges and Opportunities for India

Ankit (shifting gears as he pulls up the outline for Chapter 12, "Roadmap to Future 2044 and Beyond"): Speaking of the future, this next chapter is all about what lies ahead for India's energy journey. It's a broad look at the roadmap to 2044 and beyond. I'd love to get your thoughts on it, Saswat sir.

Saswat (intrigued, scanning the outline): This looks fascinating. If you don't mind, I'd love to jump in on this one as well. I've been thinking a lot about what the energy landscape will look like in 20 years, and we're at the tipping point where decisions made now will shape India's role globally.

Arun: Looks like we'll have another chapter with Saswat's sir signature insights.

Ankit: Definitely. Alright, let's get this one finalized and start brainstorming for what's next.

Saswat: On to the future then"

Ankit (sipping his coffee and looking around the table): So, here we are. The last chapter 'Roadmap to Future 2044 and Beyond.' I'm glad we're all together to wrap this up.

Arun: It feels like the perfect moment to take stock. We've covered so much ground, from India's geopolitical energy ties to the rise of electric vehicles. This final chapter is all about looking ahead.

Kamini: Exactly. We've discussed so many challenges, but now it's about how India can leap into the future. With all the technology advancements we've covered hydrogen, battery storage, smart grids I feel like we're standing on the edge of something big.

Rohit: Definitely. We've seen the transformation already starting. By 2044, India could be one of the world's energy powerhouses. But the roadmap is key—it has to be strategic, right from renewable energy expansion to electrification and energy efficiency.

Saswat: And we can't forget about the role of innovation. By 2044, we'll see breakthroughs in hydrogen tech, universal batteries, and P2P energy trading. The energy landscape will be completely different, and India will be at the forefront if we play our cards right.

Dr. Charusmita (smiling): Agreed, Saswat. And it's not just about the tech. We've got to ensure that the energy transition is inclusive, that it creates jobs, supports industrial development, and brings reliable energy to rural and remote areas. It's as much a social mission as it is technological.

Arun: Which means the common man has a huge role to play too. We can talk about energy independence all we want, but until households are actively part of the energy system whether through rooftop solar or smart home tech the transition won't be complete.

Ankit: Exactly! And that's why this chapter is about more than just goals for 2044. It's about the journey how we'll get there with the right mix of policies, public-private partnerships, and innovation, while also ensuring that every citizen is involved in this transformation.

Rohit (raising his cup): Well said, Ankit. To 2044 and beyond!

As India stands on the threshold of a monumental energy transition, the next two decades will determine whether it can emerge as a global leader in clean, secure, and sustainable energy.

The strides made in renewable power, electric mobility, hydrogen technologies, and grid modernization over the last decade have laid a solid foundation. But the road ahead demands an even bolder vision.

By 2044, India's energy landscape will look radically different. The country is working toward becoming energy independent, reducing its reliance on fossil fuel imports, and building a resilient system powered by renewables, advanced storage solutions, and smart infrastructure.

This vision is not just about meeting the energy demands of 1.5 billion people but also about shaping India's role as a pioneer in global climate action and green technology innovation.

This chapter brings together the threads of India's energy story from ambitious policy frameworks and technological leaps to international partnerships and community-led initiatives and maps out a comprehensive strategy for the future. It highlights the critical enablers required to achieve universal access, energy equity, and economic growth while addressing climate change head-on.

India's Vision 2044 is not merely aspirational; it is a roadmap for creating an energy-secure, inclusive, and sustainable future for generations to come.

India's Long-term Energy Strategy: Policies and Goals

India's energy landscape in 2044 is poised for a historic transformation, driven by visionary policies such as the National Energy Policy (NEP) and the broader framework of Vision 2044.

These initiatives aim to balance rapid economic growth with environmental sustainability, positioning India as a global leader in clean energy.

The cornerstone of this strategy is achieving net-zero carbon emissions by 2070 while ensuring universal energy access and affordability for a population projected to cross 1.5 billion by mid-century.

Renewable Energy Targets:

By 2044, India plans to install **over 750 GW of renewable energy capacity**, solidifying its commitment to becoming a renewable energy powerhouse. This build-out will center on solar, wind, and bioenergy, creating a diversified and resilient energy mix.

- **Solar Energy:** Solar power is expected to dominate India's renewable portfolio, with a target of 450 GW of installed capacity by 2044, including utility-scale solar parks, rooftop solar systems, and floating solar projects.

- **Wind Energy:** Wind energy will contribute an estimated 200 GW, driven by both onshore and offshore projects, particularly along India's 7,500 km coastline.

- **Biomass & Small Hydro:** Biomass and small hydro projects are projected to provide 100 GW, supporting rural electrification and grid stability.

As of March 2024, India has already achieved 175 GW of renewable energy capacity and is on track to meet its 500 GW target by 2030, laying a strong foundation for Vision 2044.

Energy Efficiency and Electrification:

Energy efficiency lies at the heart of India's strategy to meet its growing energy demand sustainably. Initiatives such as the Perform, Achieve, and Trade (PAT) scheme and the Energy Conservation Building Code (ECBC) are designed to drive a 25% reduction in overall energy intensity by 2044, particularly in energy-intensive industries like steel, cement, and chemicals.

- **Electrification of Transport:** By 2044, India aims to electrify 80% of passenger vehicles and 100% of public transport, substantially reducing oil imports and lowering urban air pollution.

- **Smart Grids and IoT Solutions:** Digitalization and automation of energy systems will optimize consumption patterns, reduce transmission losses, and integrate variable renewable energy sources more effectively.

Hydrogen Economy:

India is positioning itself as a global hub for green hydrogen production, aiming for a capacity of 10 million tonnes per year by 2044. Green hydrogen will play a pivotal role in:

- Decarbonizing heavy industry (steel, fertilizers, cement).
- Powering long-haul transport like trucks, ships, and aviation.
- Serving as an energy storage medium to balance renewable energy supply and demand.

Strategic partnerships with countries such as Germany, Japan, and Australia, alongside domestic investments from conglomerates like Reliance Industries and Adani Group, are accelerating progress toward a robust hydrogen ecosystem.

The Role of Innovation in Achieving Energy Security

Innovation is emerging as the cornerstone of India's long-term energy strategy, ensuring the country can meet its ambitious targets for energy security, affordability, and sustainability. The energy systems of 2044 will be radically transformed by breakthroughs in **battery technologies, green hydrogen, smart grids, and digital energy ecosystems.**

Advanced Battery Technologies:

Next-generation batteries such as **solid-state, sodium-ion, and aluminum-air batteries** are poised to revolutionize India's energy landscape. These innovations will be critical for:

- Scaling up electric vehicle (EV) adoption across passenger, freight, and public transport.
- Supporting large-scale renewable energy integration by providing grid balancing solutions for intermittent solar and wind power.

By 2044, India aspires to be a global leader in battery manufacturing, with an annual production capacity of 500 GWh to meet both domestic demand and export opportunities.

Universal Batteries for Energy Storage and Electric Vehicles (EVs):

A transformative concept under development is universal battery technology—standardized batteries that can seamlessly power home energy storage systems (ESS) and EVs alike.

- Consumers will be able to store excess rooftop solar power during the day and use it for household needs or to charge their EVs at night.
- This interoperability will strengthen energy independence and reduce stress on the grid during peak demand.

Universal batteries could also enable peer-to-peer (P2P) energy sharing, where households trade surplus stored energy within their communities.

Hydrogen and Fuel Cells:

Green hydrogen is set to play a pivotal role in decarbonizing industries, long-haul transportation, and energy storage. Key developments include:

- Hydrogen-powered trucks, trains, and ships, enabling low-emission logistics and trade.
- Pilot projects for hydrogen fuel cell buses in cities like Bangalore, Chennai, and Delhi, with plans for nationwide scaling by 2044.
- Hydrogen hubs integrating electrolyzers with large solar and wind farms in Gujarat and Rajasthan.

By 2044, India envisions a hydrogen economy where this clean fuel will contribute 10-15% of the national energy mix.

Smart Grids and Digital Energy Solutions:

India's power grid will undergo a technological leap with smart grid systems incorporating AI, IoT, and blockchain. These innovations will:

- Enable real-time energy management, predictive maintenance, and demand-side optimization.
- Support Time-of-Use (ToU) tariffs to encourage efficient energy consumption.
- Drastically reduce transmission and distribution (T&D) losses—from 17% in 2024 to below 6% by 2044, aligning with global best practices.

Smart grids will also empower consumers to become "prosumers" (producers + consumers), trading surplus energy in decentralized markets.

Virtual Power Plants (VPPs):

By 2044, India will have widespread adoption of Virtual Power Plants (VPPs)—cloud-based systems that coordinate thousands of small energy resources like:

- Rooftop solar panels
- Home and commercial battery systems
- Electric vehicle fleets

These VPPs will act as flexible, distributed power plants, enabling grid operators to stabilize electricity supply without relying on large centralized plants.

Public-Private Collaboration for Sustainable Energy Development

Collaboration between the public and private sectors has emerged as one of the strongest drivers of India's energy transition. By leveraging public-private partnerships (PPPs), India is fostering innovation, scaling critical infrastructure, and attracting massive investments to meet its ambitious energy targets for 2044.

These partnerships are not only accelerating renewable energy deployment but also enabling technology transfers, financing mechanisms, and capacity-building initiatives across the energy value chain.

Private Sector Investment in Renewables:

As of March 2024, private sector participation has been pivotal in expanding India's renewable energy capacity:

- **Adani Green Energy, Tata Power Renewable Energy**, and ReNew Power have collectively committed over **USD 25 billion** towards solar, wind, and hybrid energy projects over the next decade.
- Investments in **offshore wind** projects along India's western and southern coasts are gaining momentum, with private players collaborating with international partners from Denmark and Japan.
- The **Production-Linked Incentive (PLI)** scheme for advanced chemistry cell (ACC) battery manufacturing has attracted global giants like Tesla, Panasonic, and LG Chem, which are exploring large-scale battery manufacturing and energy storage facilities in states like Gujarat and Tamil Nadu.

These initiatives are expected to drive India's **renewable capacity to 750 GW by 2044**, with the private sector contributing nearly 65% of the total capacity additions.

Energy-as-Service

The **Energy as a Service (EaaS)** model is redefining how consumers and businesses interact with energy systems. Under this innovative approach:

- Consumers **pay for energy services** (like lighting, cooling, or heating) rather than purchasing energy units (kWh).
- EaaS providers install, operate, and maintain energy systems, often leveraging renewable sources and energy-efficient technologies, allowing customers to avoid upfront capital costs.

The Energy as a Service (EaaS) model, where consumers pay for energy services (such as lighting or heating) rather than for energy units, is gaining traction.

This model encourages energy efficiency and helps businesses and industries manage their energy needs more effectively. EaaS is expected to play a significant role in India's smart cities and industrial energy strategy.

Global Examples of Energy as a Service (EaaS): India can take reference from

- Schneider Electric – US and Europe

Schneider Electric, a global leader in energy management and automation, has successfully deployed EaaS solutions across commercial and industrial clients in the US and Europe. Their offerings include:

- **Energy procurement** and price optimization.
- **Energy efficiency upgrades**, such as retrofitting buildings with smart sensors and IoT systems.
- **Integration of renewable energy sources** into microgrids.

A standout innovation is Schneider's **Microgrid-as-a-Service** model, which enables companies to access clean energy without any **upfront capital investment.**

Schneider assumes responsibility for designing, financing, and operating the energy systems, while guaranteeing businesses cost savings and uninterrupted energy delivery.

- Siemens – Germany

In Germany, Siemens has pioneered the EaaS model to help meet the country's ambitious **Energiewende** (energy transition) targets. Their projects focus on:

- Smart building solutions using AI and IoT platforms for **load balancing**.
- Distributed energy systems that include solar PV, battery storage, and EV charging.
- Energy efficiency retrofits for industrial clients and large housing complexes.

Through their **Siemens Xcelerator platform**, the company provides tailored energy-as-a-service solutions, managing **entire energy ecosystems** for factories and urban spaces while helping reduce operational costs and carbon footprints.

- ENGIE – Singapore and Australia

ENGIE, a global energy giant, has demonstrated the potential of EaaS in Singapore and Australia by managing HVAC systems, renewable energy integration, and smart cooling technologies.

Key initiatives include:

- A partnership with Southeast Asia's largest real estate developer CapitaLand, delivering rooftop solar installations and energy-efficient cooling systems for high-rise buildings in Singapore.
- Supporting Australian industries in decarbonizing operations by managing their renewable energy generation and storage assets through EaaS contracts.

- GE Current – North America

GE Current, a subsidiary of General Electric, has focused its EaaS offerings on smart lighting and energy optimization for commercial properties. Their model involves:

- Retrofitting spaces with **LED lighting** and smart controls.
- Offering services on a **subscription basis**, eliminating the need for upfront costs.

This approach has enabled businesses to achieve **energy savings of up to 50%,** demonstrating how EaaS models can deliver both environmental and financial benefits at scale.

- Enel X – Italy and United States

Enel X, part of the global utility giant **Enel**, has created innovative EaaS offerings including:

- **Demand-response programs** to shift energy use during peak hours, helping businesses cut energy bills.
- **EV Charging-as-a-Service**, which enables municipalities and corporations to deploy EV charging infrastructure without capital expenditure.

Enel X's solutions are integral to **smart city projects** in Italy and urban electrification efforts in parts of the US.

India's rapid urbanization and push for **smart cities, renewable energy integration**, and industrial decarbonization create the perfect environment for **EaaS adoption**.

- For **smart cities**, EaaS can support energy-efficient street lighting, district cooling, and waste-to-energy systems.
- For **industrial parks**, outsourcing energy management allows industries to focus on core operations while achieving their sustainability targets.
- For **commercial buildings**, EaaS unlocks access to advanced energy systems without high upfront costs, fostering faster adoption of energy-efficient technologies.

By learning from global leaders like Schneider Electric, Siemens, and Enel X, India can leapfrog traditional energy models and embed sustainability deeply into its future energy ecosystem.

Collaborative Research and Development:

Joint research and development (R&D) initiatives between India's government, academic institutions, and private sector are driving transformative innovations in clean energy technologies.

Institutions like the **Indian Institute of Science (IISc), IIT Madras, and IIT Bombay** have partnered with leading corporations such as **Reliance Industries, Adani New Industries, and Tata Chemicals** to advance research in green hydrogen production, carbon capture and utilization (CCU), solid-state battery technology, and grid-scale energy storage systems.

For example, **Reliance's partnership with IISc Bengaluru** has accelerated the development of cost-efficient electrolysis technologies for green hydrogen, aiming to make India a global leader in hydrogen exports by 2035. Similarly, Adani New Industries is collaborating with global players on next-generation solar PV cells and advanced battery chemistries suited for India's climate.

These collaborations are enabling **technology localization**, reducing India's dependence on imports for critical energy equipment, and supporting the country's goal to achieve energy self-reliance by 2040.

Corporate Renewable Energy Purchases:

India's largest corporations are emerging as key enablers of the clean energy transition by committing to **100% renewable energy consumption through corporate Power Purchase Agreements (PPAs)** and self-generation initiatives.

- Infosys, a pioneer in corporate sustainability, achieved carbon neutrality in 2020 and continues to power its campuses with 100% renewable energy.
- **Wipro** and **HCL Technologies** are accelerating their adoption of renewable energy across all operations under their RE100 commitments, reducing their Scope 2 emissions significantly.
- Manufacturing giants like **JSW Steel** and **Tata Motors** are entering into long-term PPAs for wind and solar energy to decarbonize their energy-intensive operations.

This shift demonstrates how Indian businesses are integrating sustainability as a core strategy, aligning with global Environmental, Social, and Governance (ESG) benchmarks and supporting India's ambitious target of 500 GW renewable energy capacity by 2030.

By leveraging innovative financing models, corporate players are also driving investments in decentralized renewable energy systems, setting examples for medium and small enterprises to follow.

Socio-Economic Impacts of India's Energy Transition

India's energy transition is entering a decisive phase in 2025, promising to deliver far-reaching socio-economic benefits. From creating millions of new jobs to driving industrial innovation and empowering citizens, this transformation is not just about energy—it is about reshaping the nation's economy and society for decades to come.

Job Creation:

The renewable energy sector is projected to generate over 12 million jobs by 2044, spanning critical areas like solar and wind energy deployment, battery manufacturing, hydrogen production, smart grid operations, and EV ecosystem services.

As of March 31, 2025, **1.6 million direct and indirect jobs** have already been created, fueled by the surge in:

- **Solar photovoltaic installations** in rural and urban regions,
- Expansion of **EV charging infrastructure**, and
- Growing demand for **energy auditors, technicians, and smart meter specialists.**

Flagship initiatives such as the **Skill India Mission** and the **Green Skill Development Programme (GSDP)** have scaled up to train over **2.5 million workers** in emerging technologies like green hydrogen systems, grid-scale storage solutions, and next-gen EV battery maintenance.

These programs are enabling India's youth and rural workforce to actively participate in the green economy.

Industrial Development:

The energy transition is a catalyst for growth in **manufacturing, automobile production, and clean technology innovation**, positioning India as a global leader in renewable energy equipment.

By 2025, India has already become the **world's second-largest manufacturer of solar modules** (after China), with companies like **Tata Power Solar** and **Adani Solar** exporting to Africa, Europe, and Southeast Asia.

The Production-Linked Incentive (PLI) scheme for advanced battery manufacturing has drawn investments exceeding USD 7.5 billion, enabling India to expand its domestic capacity to 12 GWh per year and reduce dependence on imported battery cells.

Furthermore, India's hydrogen economy is gaining momentum. Pilot projects in green hydrogen production and ammonia export are establishing the foundation for India to emerge as a major global supplier by 2030.

Role of the Common Man:

The average Indian citizen is playing an increasingly pivotal role in the energy transition. Households are adopting:
- Energy-efficient appliances certified under the 5-Star BEE rating,
- Solar rooftop systems under the expanded PM Surya Ghar Yojana, and
- Electric two-wheelers and three-wheelers, which accounted for 2.2 million units sold between April 2024 and March 2025.

Peer-to-peer (P2P) energy trading platforms are now active in 15 Indian states, enabling rooftop solar owners to sell excess electricity to neighbors and local grids. This is fostering a decentralized and participatory energy economy.

Smart home technologies and IoT-based energy management systems are also becoming common in urban households, helping consumers optimize energy use and reduce monthly bills.

A Sustainable Energy Future: Challenges and Opportunities

India's energy transition is at a defining moment in 2025, presenting immense opportunities for growth and climate leadership, but also critical challenges that must be addressed to ensure a sustainable pathway to 2044 and beyond.

One of the foremost challenges lies in the intermittency of renewable energy sources like solar and wind, which makes maintaining grid stability increasingly complex as their share in India's energy mix rises.

By March 2025, renewables accounted for 43% of installed power capacity, but their variability underscores the urgent need for large-scale energy storage systems and advanced smart grid technologies to ensure reliable supply during peak demand periods and off-sun hours.

Affordability remains another significant hurdle. While the cost of renewable electricity has fallen to as low as USD 0.029 per kWh for solar in 2025, emerging technologies like green hydrogen and grid-scale battery storage are still expensive.

Green hydrogen production in India costs USD 2.8–3.2 per kg in 2025, with a target to bring it down to USD 1.5/kg by 2030 through innovation, scaling, and policy incentives such as the Green Hydrogen Mission Phase-II. Sustained government support, robust financing models, and public-private collaboration will be essential to make these technologies accessible and commercially viable.

The energy-water nexus also demands attention. Expanding solar power plants in arid regions like Rajasthan and Gujarat requires significant water resources for cooling and cleaning photovoltaic panels. Innovative solutions like waterless cleaning technologies and air-cooled thermal plants are being piloted to minimize the strain on local water supplies.

Yet, amidst these challenges lie tremendous opportunities for India to emerge as a global clean energy leader. By 2044, India has the potential to dominate in:

- Solar energy, targeting 450 GW of installed capacity,
- Green hydrogen production, becoming a hub for export to Europe and East Asia, and
- Battery manufacturing, supplying both domestic and international EV and energy storage markets.

The decarbonization of hard-to-abate industries such as steel, cement, and chemicals through electrification, energy efficiency, and carbon capture technologies opens new avenues for economic growth, job creation, and global climate leadership.

India's active engagement in international climate diplomacy, particularly through initiatives like the International Solar Alliance (ISA) and leadership roles at COP summits, positions the country as a crucial player in shaping the global clean energy narrative.

The International Energy Agency (IEA) projects that India will account for 28-30% of global energy demand growth by 2040, underscoring its pivotal role in the global energy landscape.

By addressing these challenges and harnessing these opportunities, India is well-poised to create a sustainable, secure, and resilient energy future, setting a model for emerging economies worldwide.

India's energy journey is entering a transformative era—one where innovation, sustainability, and inclusivity will define the nation's progress toward energy independence and climate leadership. As the country moves toward its Vision 2044, the energy sector is no longer viewed merely as a backbone for economic growth but as the very foundation for a greener, more resilient future.

With bold targets like achieving net-zero emissions by 2070, deploying 750 GW of renewable energy, and becoming a global hub for green hydrogen and battery manufacturing, India has set its sights on ambitious milestones. Yet, these goals are not just numbers they represent a commitment to providing clean, affordable, and reliable energy to every citizen, ensuring no one is left behind in this transition.

Public-private partnerships, disruptive technologies like smart grids, virtual power plants, and universal energy storage, and grassroots participation will be the drivers of this transformation. The common man's role adopting rooftop solar, energy-efficient appliances, and electric vehicles will be as crucial as government policies and industrial investments.

Challenges like grid stability, energy affordability, and the energy-water nexus remain, but India's trajectory demonstrates that with the right mix of innovation, collaboration, and strong policy frameworks, they are surmountable.

As India stands at the threshold of this energy revolution, it sends a clear message to the world: the country is not just preparing for the future it is actively shaping it.

The success of this journey will not only secure India's own energy needs but also establish it as a global leader in the fight against climate change, paving the way for a sustainable and equitable energy ecosystem for generations to come.

Well, we've reached the end of this incredible exploration into India's energy future.

You've walked with me through each chapter, from the challenges of transmission and distribution to the cutting-edge innovations in hydrogen and smart grids. But now, I want to make this even more interactive.

After all, energy security isn't just about policies and technologies; it's about you, me, and every citizen in this country. We are all players in this game

An Invitation to the Conversation

As I close this journey of words and ideas, I want to take a moment to speak directly to you the reader. Writing this book has been more than just a professional endeavor for me; it has been a personal mission shaped by my years in the trenches of India's energy sector, from manufacturing BLDC motors in my early career to witnessing first-hand the challenges and opportunities in this dynamic market.

This book was never meant to be the final word on India's energy future. Instead, it is an open invitation—a spark—to ignite conversations, debates, and collaborations about where we are headed as a nation.

India's energy story is not just about policies, technologies, or market dynamics; it's about people. It's about entrepreneurs reimagining the way we use power, engineers building smarter grids, farmers adopting solar pumps, and citizens switching to energy-efficient solutions. It's about all of us questioning, participating, and innovating.

As you turn this last page, I encourage you to share your thoughts, your experiences, and even your disagreements. Whether you are an industry veteran, a policymaker, a researcher, or simply someone passionate about India's future, your voice matters.

- What excites you most about India's energy transition?
- What challenges do you think are still under-discussed?
- How do you see your role in shaping a secure, sustainable energy future for India?

I hope this book becomes more than a collection of chapters. I hope it becomes a starting point for a larger dialogue—one that inspires action, collaboration, and bold ideas.

Let's shape India's energy story together.

I would love to hear from you. Share your thoughts, reflections, and experiences with me at:
ankit.sharma@allindiaev.com

This is not the end. It's just the beginning.
Ankit Sharma

Thank you...